GO FISHING FOR

PIKE

GO FISHING FOR
PIKE

GRAEME PULLEN

The Oxford Illustrated Press

© 1990, Graeme Pullen

ISBN 1 85509 216 6

Published by:
The Oxford Illustrated Press, Haynes Publishing Group, Sparkford, Nr Yeovil, Somerset BA22 7JJ, England.

Printed in England by:
J.H. Haynes & Co Limited, Sparkford, Nr Yeovil, Somerset.

British Library Cataloguing in Publication Data:
Pullen, Graeme
Go fishing for pike.
1. Pike. Angling
I. Title
799.1753

Library of Congress Catalogue Card Number:
90-82291

Contents

Dedication

To the legend of Loch Ken, 72lb. True or not, it fuels the imagination.

Introduction

The pike is a species of freshwater fish that has possibly more mystique surrounding it than any other fish. It is our primary predator, and because it feeds on other fish it has received a reputation it doesn't really deserve. Pike fishing has been transformed over the last twenty years into something of an art form, but prior to that, while some anglers fished for it as a sportfish, many regarded it as vermin, and therefore on the list of fish to be destroyed at all costs. In game fish rivers pike were speared, gaffed, netted or electro fished out to ensure the game fish had a better chance of survival. Now, thanks to the promotion of the pike as a highly prized species it is more protected. It still needs extensive publicity though, as large reservoirs specialising in gamefish have been known to kill pike and take them to the fish market.

Doubtless the appetite of the pike has been the cause of its earlier downfall. As recently as 1989 there was a news item in the national press about a pike in a lake having dragged a grown dog under water, chewed off three of its legs and spat out the rest. If this is the mentality of the press we still have an uphill battle to preserve it. Pike are a natural predator. In fact they are the only major predator we have in freshwater. But far from eating just anything that swims, they in fact have a role to play. Think of this. Would you rather run three hundred yards down the road to eat a meal, or simply pull up a chair to the table? While a pike will take a fish that is fit and healthy, it has a much easier job if the fish is weak or sickly and less able to escape quickly. In this respect, pike do a good job of controlling diseases in other stocks. Look at it another way. Shoal fish like roach, rudd and bream can be likened to sheep. If the water quality is right they will reproduce until there is barely enough food to support them. The instinct to breed is strong, so they keep on supplying small fish, which in turn find there isn't enough food to eat. Eventually the fish, although in adult state, become stunted, never growing beyond a certain size.

Pike can actually be stocked into a water where stunted fish exist and over a period of three years will provide not just a well balanced coarse fishery, but a superb pike fishery as well. Looking at it another way, there is no chance of the pike eating all the food fish and dominating the water—if that happened either the pike would die off because of insufficient food, or they would become stunted themselves, leaving the water full of "jack" pike of a couple of pounds. If this stage was reached there would inevitably be a few larger pike that would be capable of living off the smaller jack pike. So, from this viewpoint the pike is an important addition to any

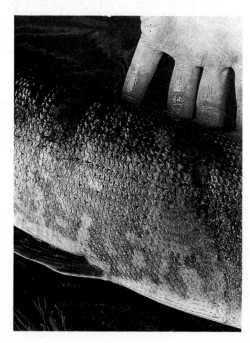

This is a 7-lb pike the author caught that has the distinctive healed over scar from being grabbed crosswise by a larger fish . . . a fish in excess of 40/50lb perhaps!

Introduction

Jerry Airey from Essex removes the hooks and bait from this small pike. If the bait is not too damaged it can be used again for another pike.

fishery, not just to provide sport for pike fishermen, but to maintain constant and healthy stocks of other species.

But pike are vulnerable too. A cold winter, rigorous spawning, high summer temperatures causing de-oxygenation and bad handling when caught are some of the problems they face. While carp and tench can live some time out of water, the pike does not fare well and bad angling techniques must account for many deaths. The fishery manager of Broadlands Lake in Hampshire confirmed this. He believes he loses up to 30% of his pike stock every year, because of losses during spawning and bad angling technique, and while he will replenish the stocks as and when he can, other clubs might not be so fortunate, so it is in the interests of the pike angler to learn the correct techniques.

Much has been written in the angling press about the correct procedure for unhooking pike. The modern pike angler should not be afraid of getting bitten by a pike. Pike feed on fish, not human fingers. Years ago pike were killed because knocking them on the

Go Fishing for Pike

The author holds hard as a good pike sheers away from the net. Never be afraid to give line at this critical stage of netting. It's far better than breaking off, or tearing the hooks out.

head to remove the hooks was far easier than fiddling about while the fish was flailing around. Many pike anglers used to allow the bait to be taken into the stomach so they were 100% sure of getting a good hookhold. If the pike was going to be eaten that was fine, but to kill them just to throw them up on the bank is sacrilege.

Modern hooking techniques should eliminate most deep hooking. The object of the exercise is to fish for sport, and if you lose the odd fish because you strike too early, that's fine, as you are going to release it anyway. My own theory is that, if you miss a pike after striking he was probably too small to get the bait in his mouth properly. It makes me feel happier!

The pike is our second largest freshwater species. It is powerful, majestic even, and should be treated with respect; today, when there is more pressure on the species than ever before, we must take care to look after what stocks we have. There are many techniques to fish for them. They live in ponds, lakes, canals and rivers. In fact

Introduction

wherever there are other fish to be eaten, the pike is likely to be. Together with the barbel, they are my favourite species, and after you have read this book you might find they become your favourite too.

About the Fish

The pike is basically a cold water fish; it is native to British waters, although in the Baltic it has been known to spawn in brackish waters. Pike tend to remain resident in a particular area and only migrate a short distance for spawning. I have found they tend to visit the same areas for spawning each year, and even the feeding areas can be the same each year as well. No doubt this is due to the proximity of weedbeds and the shelter and food they give to other fish. Locate the bait fish and the pike will be close by.

As well as being found in Europe they are known as the northern pike in America, where they also reach a good size. The Americans have the muskellunge, a fish similar to the pike, also predatory, but capable of growing very large. These are found in the Great Lakes right down to Georgia. They can be particularly spooky which strikes me as strange for a predatory fish. I remember well a musky expedition on a Pennsylvania river. We were drifting down a river looking for largemouth bass and smallmouth bass. There were musky in the river but they were rare. I had a crankbait on, better known as an Alphabet plug. I recall one cast which caught a log-like creature well into double figures. I had never seen a musky before, but knew exactly what it was. It swirled away. Twice more it followed the plug to the boat before departing completely. While they are finicky feeders I cannot help wondering if that is due to the American style of fishing predators, which is largely by artificial lures. I feel sure a nice "shiner" livebait drifted down beneath a float would have evoked a more positive response!

14

About the Fish

The tiger muskellunge is a cross breed between our own northern pike and a musky. There is always concern at the introduction of any new species but instead of importing the true musky, why not allow limited stocking of the hybrid tiger-musky? All hybrids of true species fight harder than the 'pedigree' fish so you can imagine the fight you would get from a tiger musky. And because they would probably be sterile, there would be no problem of the fish over running our own pike, or breeding to such an extent they would spread wildly throughout the country. Ask your local water authority for their opinion.

At the time of writing the world record for musky stands at 1oz under 70lb, and for the tiger musky it is 51lb 3oz. The record for northern pike on a world record status is now 55lb 1oz taken in the Lake of Grefeern, West Germany, shattering a 47-year-old record set in Savandaga Reservoir, New York. Our own British records are not to be sniffed at, with confirmed catches of just over 40lb, and several other 'monsters' which have no positive confirmation. *The Domesday Book of the Pike* by Fred Buller examines most of the really big pike captures. A 52-lb pike was supposed to have come

A double-figure pike is carried away from the water for unhooking and weighing. Always support the fish by holding the mesh and frame, avoid taking the strain on the landing net pole.

Go Fishing for Pike

Guildford angler Adrian Hutchins holds the author's 15lb 6oz Carrickmacross pike. It was one of a 200-lb catch the duo landed on a trip with Norman Haworth at Rose-Linn Lodge, Carrickmacross.

from Whittlesea Mere when it was drained in 1851, and there is the legendary head of the Loch Ken pike which was estimated around 72lb! As I mentioned previously, the pike has always had an aura of mystery surrounding it and this is reflected in folklore which tells of many monsters.

The pike is thought to live for nearly twenty years, though I doubt that with today's angling pressure many get to reach that age. They are lengthy in outline with olive green and brown backs and sides, and creamy blotches like thumbprints along the sides. The fins may have a slight pinky tinge to them, and the belly is an off white. They have a sloping flat head with eyes that are both set facing forward in a position known as binocular vision. They have hundreds of pin-like teeth on the roof of their mouths, all slanting backwards. The gill plates are large, doubtless linked with the cavernous mouth that can engulf quite substantial baits.

Having said that they inhabit virtually any type of water they do

16

in fact have a preference for the easy life. If in a river they will lie beneath or behind weedbeds. They like slack water in weirpools or alongside pilings and overhanging trees. The two main points to remember when fishing for pike are to look for still or slow-moving areas of water, and cover. Their *modus operandi* is the ambush, they tend not to chase all over the water to catch their food, they either drift near a shoal of fish slowly, or lie in wait near some sort of weedbed or obstruction. From here they can launch into their attack at a speed difficult to follow with the eye.

If they miss the food on the first strike they will not continue to chase, but settle down and strike again when a new opportunity presents itself.

Their breeding period is anything from February to April, and is largely dependent on the severity of the winter. Many of the biggest pike are caught at this time of year, but like so many records the fish are just pregnant females, the pregnancy giving them the increase in body weight. I have never been too interested in searching out a record fish. If one is fortunate enough to come my way that's fine, but I'm not prepared to continually fish for a heavily pregnant fish. To me that is akin to saying you won a judo or karate contest

A small jack pike is a good bait to fish on a large open water, when you can attach it beneath a vaned float to drift it out long distances.

with an eight-month pregnant mother! Hardly an achievement, so I enjoy catching the smaller, hard scrapping fish that have either spawned, or have yet to spawn.

Pike are thought to pair up for breeding purposes, but I have seen as many as four or five small male "jack" pike surrounding one female. Whether there is a final pairing at the last moment I couldn't honestly say. Their eggs are sticky and adhere to weed stems where they stay until they hatch after about three weeks. Again temperature may dictate an early or late hatch. They then feed on a yolk sac for about a week, after which time they will eat anything living they can, going straight into the food chain as our primary predator.

They feed almost entirely on fish but are not averse to tadpoles, frogs, toads or chicks. While I treat all tales such as mules being dragged in by their lips as they drank at the river with disdain, I did witness, along with friends a big pike trying to pull a full grown mallard duck down, while we were barbel fishing in the Trammels section of the Royalty. There is a sidestream coming in there, and it used to be good for roach, chub and bream, with the slack between the two waters making an ideal place for a big pike. Later that winter a pike was caught at about 34lb, and I feel sure this was the same fish.

Doubtless the 'ferocity' of the pike and its legendary reputation account for the following it has had over the years. As long ago as 1854, Robert Blakey wrote: "pike fishing has become of late years a very fashionable and general branch of angling". One of the legends reported by Izaak Walton in the *Compleat Angler,* was that pike were in fact bred from a weed called pickerel-weed and another glutinous substance somehow fused together by the sun's heat. Although this is a way out theory it probably originated from an angler watching pike spawn in a thick weed bed, taking out a handful of weed and seeing the eggs, which as I previously mentioned were sticky, and realising that after a warm spring the same weedbed was full of miniature pike! That theory I can find a logical explanation for.

But what about a species of pike called the pickerel? I have caught them in the tiny ponds and lakes along the Cape Cod

Small pickerel like this cape cod fish rarely grow large, but have very similar markings to our northern pike.

peninsula near Boston, USA, and they are reputed to like colder water in the northern States. They certainly do not run to any size; the largest specimen I can trace is the 8-lb class world record which stands at just 7lb 4oz. While it is found only in the United States, its Latin name is *Esox Niger* (Leseur, 1818). If Izaak Walton mentioned pickerel weed there must surely be some sort of link between the two? With the limited growth rate of this species I can see no point in adding it as a proposed new species for British pike anglers. While our own northern pike may be considered a prolific breeder, possibly laying thousands of eggs, they too are subject to predation by water fowl and eels. Mortality rates are always high in any egg laying situation where thousands are laid, and you would be mistaken if you thought that once the pike is a week old and starting on the miniature food chain that he is invincible. Even up to a weight of 8lb I have taken pike that bear the mark of an attack by a larger fish, though when they are half a pound to a pound must be their most dangerous time as their weight then corresponds with that of the food fish. The larger they grow the more chance they have of surviving.

Go Fishing for Pike

Of growth rates, a standard cannot be found. Some pike anglers thought they could grow up to 4lb in a year, but this must be relative to their adult weight. A three pounder surely cannot achieve that much growth without intensive feeding, while a twenty pounder might take a 4-lb chub in one meal! Much depends on the quality of food they are living on. A pike living in the spartan waters of an acid Irish lough would be unlikely to achieve much growth rate with stunted perch as its main diet. In contrast, a pike living in a trout stillwater with high-protein bait fish on which to feed, would do much better.

Much depends also on how much energy the pike has to expend in catching its prey. If it strikes at, and catches a 2-lb bream it will probably not feel the pangs of hunger for two or three days, and will therefore not be expending much energy over that period. Far from being the vicious murderers of fish they were painted to be even fifty years ago, they simply take what they require to satisfy their appetite. If there are no large bait fish they will eat more of the smaller fry. A good spawning from other coarse fish presents itself as a readily available food supply in a confined area, but the protein benefit from grabbing a two-inch-long roach fry is obviously not the same as that from a one-pound, high-protein trout. The energy expended in the catching of such small fish will mean the pike will feed for a longer period as his energy reserves are burnt up quicker by having to continually strike at small fish. Several times I have been fishing for pike and seen them suddenly flash through the swim to grab a 2-lb chub from my line. On light tackle it will invariably break off and eat the chub. But the disappointment for me is that I will be unlikely to catch that pike even if I fish for it. Having fed on a big fish it will skulk off to the nearest slack or weedbed to digest it over a couple of days.

In contrast, if I am knocking out small roach and get one taken by a pike on the way in, I have every confidence of landing that fish by using another roach bait. When pike feed on smaller fish I am far happier than when they pick off a large individual specimen. Many pike anglers feel that the bigger the pike, the bigger the prey they feed on. In my experience this may not be so, a large pike merely indicates that it has the *capacity* to take a large fish. It may

About the Fish

Big pike will take big fish, of that there is no question. On a recent bream trip to Ireland, Graeme's fishing partner, Norman Wilkinson had this 2-lb bream attacked by a huge Shannon river pike. It was estimated at well over 30lbs. The Bream's spine was severed by just one row of the pike's teeth. The pike's jaws were so large they completely missed the outside edge of the tail!

be in a water full of 8-oz roach, but it can still grow to a large size.

The colouring of the pike makes it attractive to look at. Those cream flank markings can be most vivid on a pike that has never been caught before. While some pike anglers believe the markings correspond to the environment in which the fish lives, I believe simply that some fish have more markings than others through some genetic imprint. That they stand out vividly is just a sign that the pike in question is in tip-top condition, confirmed by the deep olive green back that positively shines in a healthy fish.

The fact that the pike launches itself in a single attack at a fish ensures that from the moment he kicks into top gear from a standing start, he is totally committed. For that reason alone the angler will do well to try artificial lures, as properly fished, and taking advantage of the latest lure patterns, it is a fun way to catch pike.

Location

Large pike, which most anglers want to catch, can turn up at almost any type of water where there is sufficient food to maintain them. That means rivers, ponds, lakes and reservoirs. As with all species of fish, the key to success is location, whether you are looking for a large single pike, or an area where small to medium sized fish roam. It largely depends what you want. During the late 1960s there were a lot of bags of good pike being caught from low double figures up to twenty pounds. This was due to anglers joining together in small groups of three to ten, and pooling all their information about where they thought the pike would be. Some used more than the usual two rods, and this, although possibly outside the ruling of the relevant water authority, was called saturation fishing. Obviously with more anglers fishing in a concentrated effort, more larger pike were located more quickly. Huge catches were made, the resultant publicity bringing even more pike anglers to the scene. Pike as I mentioned before, cannot sustain heavy angling pressure, and the easy fishing of that period is now a thing of the past. The popularity of the sport gained momentum, and while the dedicated pike angler would fish the year through anyway, it was the pleasure angler who suddenly became aware that his casual weekend trip had more than a passing chance of success if he fished where these groups had been, that put the pressure on.

It wasn't long before, in popular places like the fens, anglers were following the cars of the successful anglers in an effort to find out where they were catching the fish. So much for the brotherhood of

22

the angler. The result of this intensive pressure was that the pike spread out, and good fishing suddenly became harder to find. Then location was more of a key to success than actual technique or bait presentation.

Rivers

I think I can safely dispense with brackish water, for although pike may visit there, most anglers will not. That leaves two main types of water: running water or still water. Of the two, I feel the hardest fighting pike come from the rivers. Some say it is because they had to be well muscled fish to hold their station in the current, but as mentioned before, pike will always find the easiest place to settle in, with the minimum of effort. I think it is just the current itself that makes them seem as though they fight harder. In a fast shallow trout stream you can hook a low double-figure pike on a plug and suddenly find yourself attached to a fish that takes off like a yellowfin tuna! I would be the first to say, that size for size, the pike is not the best species for stamina. Some fish scrap harder than others of course, and those that rarely if ever, feel the sting of the hook, scrap hardest. Having previously mentioned the key to success being location, this is never more true than on a river.

I have spent quite some time trying to locate the bigger pike in clear rivers like the Kennet, Lower Stour, and Hampshire Avon. The best time for observation is during the summer months when the water is at its lowest level, and the sun is at its peak giving surface penetration of light. On a still day I can spot many of the pike, but a good deal of the river is totally devoid of them. It might be suggested that a pike cull is undertaken as part of a gamefish protection policy, and therefore the pike numbers are limited. Even allowing for that, the pike I do spot are invariably downstream of any concentrations of baitfish. The water pace is slow or steady, and they rarely move up into any fast water.

The only time I've seen them do this is when I have been groundbaiting a swim for barbel and chub all day, and the small fish are concentrated in that area. Even then the pike do not move into the swim until late afternoon. I believe this is due to their high visibility in summer allowing the baitfish time to dart into the safety of the nearest weedbed. With low light levels the pike has more success of launching a profitable attack so you can see that fishing in late afternoon during summer optimises your fishing time.

In contrast, the winter offers a couple of variables. First the baitfish will tend to move into deeper, slower reaches of the river where temperatures remain constant, and energy can be retained in the slower current. The pike will require the same conditions and therefore be close by. The light conditions will also be lower so their success when striking at the baitfish will be that much greater. These are a couple of tips that you won't read in any other book, and it could put you an extra fish on the bank.

As for areas to look for in the river, much will depend on the pace of the current. In a deep, slow-moving river the pike can hole up anywhere along its length, although you must try and find some baitfish. In fast rivers they will, as mentioned before be close to

Pike love ambush territory, and even in winter these sunken trees and inflow ditch are typical of ground worth covering.

food, but they have a preference for hanging around anywhere they can find cover for ambush. Weedbeds must be high on your list of priorities. One of the best places is in an area of slack water, possibly an eddy, or unused sidestream where lilies have died back. In summer this place may be totally unfishable, but in winter the pike love to rest in the stems of the dying lilies waiting to zip out and snatch any passing fish.

The tail end of streamer weed is another place to look for pike. Often, although an area of river looks choked with streamer weed, the gravel underneath is clear. The weed just grows from a main root and flows downstream in the current like hair. Small fish find sanctuary under this, and the pike will be found on the downstream end of this weed.

They will also lie below weir sills, rather than the main sluice. Water in a river runs faster on the surface than it does at the bed, which the pike find to their liking. Slow water means they have to burn up less energy to stay "on station", and weir sills in particular have a slack water area directly beneath the fall-off. It might look fast, but it is a good area to try with both baits and artificials. The drawback with weir sills is that they often get debris and branches washed onto them during floods. If any logs or branches get caught on the concrete sill as a flooded river drops they become water-logged until the next flood lifts them off and dumps them over the edge of the sill. Instead of floating down the river they spill over the sill edge and sink to the bottom. Here they make great places for bait fish and pike alike, but represent a tackle graveyard to the pike angler. Be prepared to lose some gear in such places. To avoid losing valuable lures it might pay you to make a couple of casts with a lead and draw it over the bottom to locate any snags. With weir sill fishing you can even throw the bait or lure up onto the sill itself if not covered with silkweed, and twitch it off to fall quietly in the water. Start your retrieve back early as pike have a tendency to hit near the surface in this highly oxygenated water.

Alongside the weir sills you have the main sluice. In my ex-perience this is never the best place for pike as the turbulence is too strong, but fish either side of the main power fall and you can find them. There is also a slack area directly beneath and behind where the main flow gushes in. If you cast into the rushing water your bait will soon get swept downstream. By using extra weight you can drop through the main rush of water and reach the quiet area under the sluice. I won't say you get a lot of pike there, but it is certainly an area worth checking out when weirpool fishing.

Also worth trying is the tail end of the main sluice flow where the current pace starts to ease up. This is good for most fish as the flow brings food to them, and during summer the fish will congregate here for the higher oxygen content. If I have any favourite spot in a weirpool for pike, it must be where the weir sluice shoots the main

The binocular vision of the pike can be seen by the eye location of this big fish. This means they have to turn their whole body at an angle to see baitfish at the rear. Once targeted however, the binocular vision makes an excellent "sight" for grabbing any fish moving in front of its field of vision. The author undertook his own tagging programme in the early 1970s. His opercular tag can be clearly seen on the trailing edge of the pike's gill cover. A National tagging programme might benefit the future of the species, and verify to what extent angling pressure affects the pike.

flow to one side. This leaves a larger slack water area on one side than it does on the other. The circulating current is scarcely perceptible, but it can hold several pike, possibly dozens if the weir is on a large river.

I used to spend a lot of time fishing Thames weirpools, particularly at Pangbourne, upstream from Reading in Berkshire. I did quite a lot of tagging in this weirpool when in my late teens and early twenties, and often wonder if a twenty pounder will be caught here bearing one of my opercular tags. I always fish alone when possible, and at that time had the entire weirpool to myself. I could move the boat about until I found the best taking areas, and surprisingly more were caught in the main weirpool than in the island channels below. I would have expected the main bags of pike to come from the slower reaches of river downstream several hundred yards, but probably 90% of my fish came in the main weirpool.

It was also in this weirpool that Adrian Hutchins hooked what I believe was one of the biggest river pike ever! We were spinning by an overhanging tree and the area was a nightmare for losing lures. Retrieve too near the top and we got nothing; too near the bottom and the boughs of an old chestnut would snag you every time.

Adrian was nearing the snag. Slower and slower he retrieved as the takes were few and far between. We were in the boat, and I actually saw his rod tip drag over. He struck, nothing happened, swore as he thought he was snagged, then shouted as the snag moved off. It was my best spinning rod and it took on a curve I had never seen in it before. It was an incredibly slow moving fish, indicative of weight, so I upped the anchor and we drifted around the pool being towed by this unseen fish. He made absolutely no impression on it at all, and after fifteen minutes my estimation of its weight was well over 30lb! A crowd gathered on the car park, and pub regulars turned out, pints in hand. The few turns of line Adrian did gain were wrenched from the spool in powerful lunges. He passed me the rod and I hauled away. I made no impression at all. After a further few minutes the line rose towards the surface, I readied what was obviously an inadequate net, and . . . the hooks pulled out! I still think that was an incredible fish, certainly the biggest I have seen hooked up. Despite many years spent searching that weirpool since, and a high mortality rate of expensive lures and baits because I wanted to fish as close to the snag as possible, I never hooked him again.

When I concentrated my efforts on the aforementioned areas of weirpools I have had up to twenty fish into double figures in just one session. They would come to a wide variety of baits and techniques, but one of the favourite areas I found them in was around the steel or concrete weir pilings. These are put into the water to prevent bankside erosion, either where the main run of water hits the first bank from leaving the sluice, or on the outside of a bend in the river where the increase in current pace might wear the bank away. Quite why these areas are good holding ground for pike I cannot say, but the same applies for finding salmon. The latter obviously like the faster flow, but pike as mentioned before, tend to lie in a steady current or slack. It can only be the dark background provided by the pilings that allow the pike to blend in and launch an attack from this ambush point that attracts them. The only other theory I have heard is that the outside of the bend, having the fastest water, will swing any dead fish straight into the pike's vision.

Pilings rarely hold snags due to the fast current sweeping any debris away, so you can fish any bait or lure close to the metal work without fear of snagging too often.

The final place I would look for pike in a river is the sidestream from the junction where it enters the river to a point about twenty yards downstream. Coarse fish use sidestreams both for spawning in the summer and for getting out of the main flow when the winter floods are coming down. Rarely will there be too many pike actually up the sidestream, except in low water winter conditions. They are more likely to lie at the entrance, just on the edge of the main flow, drifting into the slower water when the small fish are most active. Even the slightest water meadow drainage stream or even a ditch, provided it is not connected to any farm run-off effluent, can be holding places for the pike.

A similar situation exists on a larger scale when you start to look for pike in the big Scottish and Irish lochs. In Ireland especially, many lakes and lochs are connected with a system of small rivers, and where this river enters a loch is a good place to try. In spring the coarse fish like roach and bream will be moving into the rivers either to spawn or clean off, or even migrate up to the next loch. This concentration of food fish will draw the pike, so treat any streams or rivers running into a large body of water as you would the sidestream. Most of your takes should come right at the entrance, or slightly to the downstream bank of the loch where the river flow peters out.

I remember losing a monstrous pike one spring at Ballinamore. I forget which river I was fishing but I had reached the point where it ran into the loch. I had already taken some fish to about 7lb on a plug, firing it out to the far bank and letting it swing round slowly in the peat coloured water before retrieving. It was strewn with boulders near the mouth of the loch and I was carefully avoiding the bigger boulders. There was a boil behind my plug, an arm-wrenching pull and I was fast into a fish that ripped line from the reel in a downstream rush the like of which I had never experienced in pike fishing before. The drag was squealing and I was back winding as well. With around 120 yards of line gone I crashed through the undergrowth, rod held high, trying to keep pace with the pike. No chance. It careered off into the lake, hung a left and my line came out from the water and up the bank as the fish cut the corner!

Inevitably perhaps, the line popped. Had I been told this story by some other angler I would have described it as a foul hooked fish, with the hooking point near the tail. This situation leaves any fish free to swim hard, giving a fight far in excess of its actual size. However I had seen the boil on the surface as the lure was taken so am quite confident the fish was mouth hooked.

Canals

Canals are not my favourite pike haunt but they can offer the odd good fish so they are worth mentioning. Even for other species of coarse fish I have difficulty in accepting a narrow canal can throw up huge bags of fish. But then you would be sitting in one place waiting for the fish to come to you. When pike fishing a canal, you would do better to go to the fish. Sticking in one swim is alright if you know the area to be a hotspot for pike, but if it is a canal you have not fished before, or have only sketchy experience on, the roving technique is likely to produce more confident results. Location again is the key. For that you should find a stretch that is match fished fairly heavily. This will at least let you know the stretch holds a good number of small fish; if it wasn't, it wouldn't be a prime match venue.

Having found maybe a half or mile-long stretch of towpath, work your way along covering the water with either lures or deadbaits, casting to the far bank and working back towards you. I would suggest you do no more than three fan-shaped casts, before moving down about twenty yards. It might pay you to throw a live or deadbait with one rod, and cover the water with another rod using either twitched deadbait, or artificial lure. Only by covering the water like this can you hope to find a feeding pike. If you hook one, give that area an extra fifteen minutes of your time as there may well be another fish in the area.

The only other area worth looking into is the 'flash', or turning area used by the old canal boats. Many canals, although not used by the barges of yesteryear, are used by boaters. With restoration in mind, many canal societies embark on dredging campaigns, and the turning bays are excavated as well. This proves a useful area for both small fish and pike, maybe even allowing you to knock out a few small roach for fresh livebait. They won't be always in the flash; sometimes they migrate up and down the main canal section following the baitfish. But try the flash first before moving away, as it is obviously like an oasis in the desert to fish.

Stillwaters

For stillwaters you have the choice of two: either the regular lake normally associated with fishing clubs and private estates, or the more familiar gravel pits. Both are capable of throwing up large individual specimens, or bags of fish. The first waters I cut my teeth on were estate lakes, simply because I live in a part of Hampshire

Location

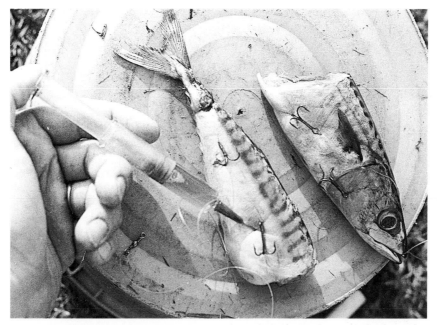

Half mackerel deadbaits are very good for picking up the larger pike. Here the author injects a mackerel tail with pilchard oil, to leave a scent trail in the water.

that has plenty of estates. Then I graduated on to the gravel pits, which around twenty years ago were coming into their own. Of the two I would suggest the large open gravel pit is more likely to produce big pike, simply because a newly formed pit has a growth rate potential that will be on the increase, as opposed to the estate lake, where it might be on the decline.

I was bailiff of Dogmersfield Lake near Odiham for many years when I was in my late teens, and often had the water to myself. The largest pike to come out then was a 36 pounder; few knew about that I can tell you! The lake was not large, but it was the one water I came to know really intimately. I would fish it on Sundays, then maybe twice a week from November to March. Prior to that it was often choked with weed, depending on what vegetable the farmer up the hill was growing, and more importantly, what chemical he was treating them with. A year of potatoes meant the green weed bloom would be considerable, and no fishing could be done until Novem-

Go Fishing for Pike

Proof of the pudding: the author with a nice "twenty", plus another double at his feet, taken on the mackerel head and tail sections in the previous picture!

ber. The estate lake was shallow at one end, about six feet or less at its deepest point. There were no lilies, and it was getting silted up. Just over the hill was Tundry Pond; the two lakes were steeped in history as carp waters used by the monks, linking both to Fleet pond. I fished alone, caught literally hundreds of pike, and did most of my tagging there. Dogmersfield lake also gave me my first double, about 10lb 6oz, and I recall to this day leaping up and down screaming with delight as the pike flopped about in the muddy net.

The problem with estate lakes is that they were deeper eighty years ago than they are today. Many are silted up, and the removal of silt is an expensive operation with current dredging costs. They have a soft muddy bottom, which means together with their shallow depth, they are susceptible to wave action. Our prevailing wind is south-westerly, so the northern end of any estate lake is likely to be the deepest, with silt dislodged by wave action, and the southern end the shallowest. Obviously this does not apply to tiny estate ponds sheltered by woodland, but generally waters around 50 acres or more conform to this pattern. The southern end, being the shallowest should be where the greatest weed growth is, so don't discount water even a couple of feet in depth if there are weedbeds around.

In summer the fish will be spread out all around an estate lake, but once the colder water temperatures come in late autumn and through the winter, the predator and prey move into the north end where it may be deeper. If the estate lake is an open-water venue with little shelter in it, you will have to look for any kind of weedbed or "structure" to help locate both pike and food fish. If the estate is set with woodland around it, check out the areas with overhanging branches. Willows in particular are noteworthy as the roots often extend out under the surface. In summer the roach and rudd will lay their eggs on the root fronds, and the pike are quite likely to be close by. In the winter, the fry hatched from those same eggs will need some sanctuary, and they will hang around any roots and tree branches in the water. Again, the pike will be close by. They can also lie in wait amidst the tangle of branches to launch an attack on any passing fish. Even a branch stuck out in the centre of a lake will prove an attraction to the baitfish. Having fished around the world I actually dumped some branches out in the north end of Dogmersfield lake to provide such cover, or "structure" as the Americans called it. I took several fish from around it, but once the water rose I hauled them out to regain my lost tackle and to prevent anglers from snagging on it. Introducing structures into a lake is worth considering by any club or syndicate interested in running a proper pike fishery. But remember to map or buoy it to mark where it is!

Some estate lakes have inflow and outflow streams. These can vary in size from a small ditch to a slow moving stream. Both can attract pike. Many estate waters were constructed by landscapers, and were formed simply by damming an existing stream, and building up the surrounding land to form a bank. If there was a natural depression in the land this saved on additional banking. This accounts for many estate lakes being of uniform depth as they conform to the contours of the land prior to flooding. In large lakes there may still be some flow from the river, pushing in a narrow channel down the lake. It spreads more the farther it is from the inflow.

Sometimes an underground spring breaks through the lake bed and this attracts fish, especially in hot weather. A warm summer in such shallow water produces a low oxygen content. Any area that offers both more oxygen and cooler temperatures brings in both baitfish and the pike. Therefore I suggest fishing these old river bed areas in high summer, which should give you just the tiny edge you need for success.

The small ditches that may feed a smaller estate lake are likely to dry up in high summer so have no immediate influence on temperature or oxygen content. Nevertheless in winter, when they do run in, they can draw fry and therefore pike with their fresh water. Looking at the other end of the system from the outflow, in a large water it will invariably have a "draw" on it. Any food items floating on the surface will gradually be pulled towards the outflow and so spill over into the stream. If you fish after a good south-westerly blow in the autumn there will be a surfeit of leaves and debris on the water. If you go a step further and fish a couple of days *after* the water has flooded, and is dropping, that same debris will not be gushing over the sluice of the outfall into the river, but will be very likely drifting into a corner where it will form a scum and leaf cover for small fry to hide under. Another good pike area. As you can see using all these small pointers I can establish immediately where I am going to fish, given the weather conditions.

Estate waters offer a good place for the piker to try, whether they are privately owned and permission is needed before entry, or whether an angling club is leasing the rights. The water depth is uniform, and of course you can take pike anywhere on the lake, as well as from the hotspots I have mentioned. In contrast to the even depth of these estate lakes you can also try any of the numerous gravel pits that provide so much of our modern fishing.

The gravel pit system was born out of a need to build our motorway system. Thus wherever there is a motorway, there is likely to be some gravel pits close by. Sometimes there is one large pit, at other times as many as a dozen small pits are dug. Gravel pits probably form the backbone of freshwater fishing in the southern half of England, and produce an amazing array of different species.

You can also groundbait an area for pike. Here the author injects pilchard oil into the centre of these golf-ball-sized pellets. They can be catapulted long distances, and as small fish nibble away the groundbait they release the oil, which together with their own vibrations, attract the pike.

Two factors need to be considered when looking at these waters: the method used in the excavation of the gravel, and how long ago the fish stocking was done.

One of the more popular methods of creating small pits was the "throwback" technique. This left the contour of the lake bed in sharp rises and deep hollows which, when filled with water, allowed weed to grow quickly, fry to flourish, and big fish to grow bigger. The advantage of a newly flooded gravel pit is that the fish can grow very quickly. The entire food chain is boosted by a newly flooded water, and while pike may not initially benefit from this, they will appear in both size and numbers as the head of coarse fish grows. A pit with plenty of bars and shallows allows for easier baitfish location, while the large open water makes things a bit more difficult.

The large pit may also enjoy a flourishing food and fish chain, but isolation of species may be more difficult. The depth of the large pit depends on how successful the gravel extraction was. If it is a deep water, say down to twenty feet or more, there will be good margin fishing. This is where the bank has been eroded by wave action to form a small ledge about three feet or more, before dropping away to the deep water. Both fry and pike will patrol this area, and chances are good for baits or lures cast parallel to the bank. This deep water will possibly be very clear, and weed growth heavy due to concentrated light penetration. Many of the weedbeds may just be floating mats which are not necessarily conducive to attracting fish. These pits are best fished in autumn and winter.

The smaller pits, to my mind are easier for fish location. I have stressed before the importance of locating structure, and if there are no weedbeds or overhanging trees about, then the gullies between the gravel bars do the same job. These gullies are like underwater valleys and the shoals of coarse fish move along them in their quest for food. Up on the top of gravel bars the temperature will be warmer, the weed growth thicker and the food more prolific. Therefore, the greatest activity is likely to be on the gravel shelf. While I have taken pike from the top of gravel bars it has generally been during the summer months when I have been covering the pit with various plugs.

Location

A seriously B-I-G pike! This monster was taken by Mr Lotnar Louis, and weighed in at an incredible 55lb 1oz (Photo: courtesy I.G.F.A Florida/Jan Eggars).

In the autumn and winter any activity on the gravel bars is likely to be on the lower edge of the sloping drop off. I suggest sticking to these areas primarily because a newly filled gravel pit is likely to be devoid of any bankside cover. With all that heavy machinery churning around it can take a couple of years before it grasses over with scrubland and weeds. If run by an angling scheme, small saplings may be planted in the bankside. Another couple of years and the water will be producing both good fishing and good bankside cover. Initially those deeps between gravel bars will be the place to fish, but once the shrubs start to overhang the water you again have structure which will isolate fish. Many times I have taken pike in the margins, only six inches from bankside grass that was hanging a few inches in the water. Pike love to use any sort of cover, and I think they know they can merge against the background of a muddy bank better than if they were drifting around mid-water. If you have overhanging trees so much the better as roach fry in particular love to hang around the fringes of this. If coupled to deep water you could have a hotspot in the making, especially if the prevailing south-westerly breeze pushes into that area.

Following on from the depths, gravel bars and overhanging structure, you should pay particular attention to promontories and bays. A portion of land jutting out on a pit may be where the "throwback" extraction technique has been used, and waste has been piled up to form this promontory. The area directly in front of you is likely to shelve away evenly, with deeper water to either side. From the end of a peninsula you can therefore fish gullies on either side. A headland on an otherwise barren gravel pit will allow you to drift floatfished baits out over a wider area.

If the pit has some bays, check out those facing the prevailing south-westerly airflow. Take a compass to check bearings if you have never fished a venue before, but remember the actual wind direction may be changed by winds swirling around trees and woodland. Wait until a westerly or southerly is blowing then check to see where all the ripples are blowing. This can also be a productive area, regardless of depth as the food drifts into here, followed by small fish, followed by the pike.

Small bays that can be reached by walking are simple to fish, but there may be a bay on the opposite side of a large pit, with bankside vegetation preventing you from getting to it. If long casting is out of the question, then you must approach it with either live or dead baits. Lures cannot be fished. Use either a balloon, secured by a release clip, or one of the many drifter floats available on the market. If possible get a boat to reach the spot. I once covered a pike match when qualifying events were being held at different venues throughout the country. While I covered the event in my capacity as photographer-reporter, it also gave me a good insight into where the fish were coming from. This was invaluable when it was a water I had no previous experience of. One of the gravel pits at the Yateley complex, famous for carp captures, and about 3 miles from my home hosted a pike qualifying match. I wandered around and stood behind the person who eventually won the event. It wasn't what he netted that impressed me, but the number of fish he

Location

When you find a bottle neck of small fry you simply have to hit the area for as long as it lasts. The author went on to land over 90lb of pike and quickly returned this massive haul to the water. Note the fish have all been laid on wet plastic. There is no need to retain pike unless you want a specific photograph, or are involved in a pike match.

lost. I had been told there were only a few pike in the water, but as it had been used for match fishing there had been a substantial injection of small fish. All good food for any pike in the water.

The peg from which the winning catch came, was in between some overhanging trees right at the bottom end of the water where the prevailing breeze blew. It was a classic area for any angler experienced at reading the water for signs of fish. Small fry were bottle-necked in this bay, the only sanctuary being the margins where the trees grew into the water. I was in the swim two mornings later, for a quick two-hour session before work. Success was immediate and I took a couple of pike, missing three others. That was on twitched dead rudd. There were so many fry bottled up in the bay that the pike refused to look at an artificial, only took a deadbait half-heartedly, but went for livebaits with gusto. I prefer not to fish at busy weekends because any good catch is soon noted and then it is difficult to get that pitch again. Nevertheless on this particular occasion I hit the swim on a Sunday morning. I decided to use small livebaits lip-hooked on a single treble. The ripple was pushing into the bay from a warm and wet westerly airflow. Water temperatures were high. By lunchtime I hadn't moved from the bay, which was barely fifty feet across. I had tipped off a colleague Adrian Hutchins, that I was likely to "do the business" and he turned up around 2pm with the cameras. He had two other pike anglers in tow who were fishing for big pike in the car park pit. Both had blanked. It's a bit difficult to play things down when your landing net is covered with slime and your rod is hooped over into another pike! We laid out the plastic sheeting to protect the fish, and weighed up, following with a quick photo session. "Bloody Hell" said one of the lads, "how long have you been keeping this quiet?" I didn't think he'd believe it was only my second session on the pit. That haul of pike was finally to finish at around 90lb and as we slid them back, my float went away again and I landed another low double! Thus you can see that location is the key to successful piking.

While gravel pits offer the most opportunities for piking to the average angler, it is only fair to say that the wild open lochs of Ireland and Scotland offer the largest bodies of water. My own experience of fishing these truly enormous waters is limited to Ireland, and I confess to being bitten by the bug that drives a special sort of pike angler to search the waters for some of the enormous pike that inhabit them. Here, the art of location is made much more difficult by the vastness of the body of water being searched. Yet the loneliness of these wild waters make them seem almost magical. Catching a floppy old backend female pike from a hard-fished gravel pit is completely different from catching a leaping, head-shaking "wild" pike from the big waters that may possibly have never felt the sting of the steel before. Too many blank sessions on these big waters however can set your brain in free spool, and while I love to troll them, I still return to the small waters for a booster of easier pike, just to reassure myself that I can still catch a few. After a few of these blank sessions you begin to appreciate the single-minded anglers who dedicate their lives to fishing their way round the lochs in search of fishy areas. And it is not just the surface area that creates the location problems, but the depths as well. Water over 60 feet deep may have limited life in its layers, but you can never really say if there is a big pike skulking around or not.

Having said that however, use the same location technique as mentioned before. If the loch in question has coarse fish as the main prey for pike, look for weedbeds on the edge of any drop off. If you are searching for a pike full of spawn to give you the heaviest weight try the shallow bays in early springtime. Yet if the loch has a head of gamefish like salmon or trout you must look to the river mouth, or entrances where feeder streams and ditches run in. All may attract the gamefish at varying times of year, and doubtless the pike will be close by.

Out in the centre of the loch you may have to locate shoals of coarse fish like perch, using an echo sounder. There might be certain areas of water that are warmer than others and the baitfish shoal up, hanging in suspended animation at one depth. It is doubtful they are feeding then, but any bulk of baitfish will attract the attention of predators. Just as lions, wild dogs and cheetahs track the vast migrating herds of Wildebeest on the Serengeti plain in Africa, so the shoals of baitfish are tracked down by the pike. Find one, and the other shouldn't be far away.

Fishing this big water can be done in two ways. You can go to a river mouth, bay or general area where you think, or have heard the pike will be. Invariably you will be in a bout, so you can either anchor or drift, working the area thoroughly to find the pike, using either baits and lures. The other method is to troll, either with oars or outboard, pulling baits or lures behind you. If you search the deep water you will need an echo sounder, and if you want to fish baits or lures deep you must use a downrigger. This latter method is for me, more satisfying than copying someone else's success just to make short cuts. If you have searched a large area then obtained a strike in an unknown place you can really say that fish is yours, and that for me is the ultimate in pike fishing.

While many lakes and gravel pits are so hard fished the pike are caught several times over and the ceiling weight of the venue is established, a big open loch has untapped potential. Many of our biggest ever pike have come from open waters, and little is known about their true content as so few anglers really fish them. Pike feeding on gamefish are likely to reach the largest sizes, so a loch with migratory or non-migratory gamefish is surely the best prospect for a big fish. However, some reservoirs held over as brown and rainbow trout fisheries offer tremendous potential for record pike as there is always a constant injection of fresh, high-protein feed in the shape of thousands of trout stocked from trout farms. Any pike in such a water will pack on weight fast, as we have seen from Llandegfedd reservoir in Wales where a test fishing on the trout water yielded no less than four pike in excess of 40lb including the recent 1990 new British record.

There is every likelihood of this, or a similar water producing an 'instant' record pike, but to my mind the only record that counts would be a truly wild fish from one of the big open lochs where few anglers visit. The popularity of trying for a record pike can be seen from the numbers of anglers rushing to fish these waters. Big pike hold a mystery of their own, and it is worth noting that many of our legendary monster pike catches have come from the wild open waters of Scotland and Ireland.

So you can see, catching pike is largely down to the location of the species, after that it is comparatively easy. Plus you can see there are many different types of water in which you can catch them, the last of which must be the slow-moving rivers and drains of East Anglia. Here the location of the pike is made easier in a sense because the drainage system for the agricultural land means there is plenty of pike water available within one long cast to the far bank. The drawback is that you may have to travel many miles up or down the drain systems until you find the pike. Such drains are prolific for shoals of coarse fish, but even these can go on long migrations up and down the drain depending on weather and water conditions. There are also areas known to many locals and regulars that are good all season, the baitfish and pike seldom moving. However angling pressure is such that even these tiny "oases" soon get known, and receive a lot of attention. 'Structure' in the shape of trees or weedbeds may be limited. The bottom contour is likely to be uniform and constant, with perhaps a ledge before the deepest central channel. In summer the baitfish will be in close, and the pike

Location

Another double being weighed up by the author. Always support the bulk of the pike's body in a proper weigh sling, and deduct any weight of a wet weigh sling from the total weight.

near them. In the colder weather they tend to run up and down the edge of the shelf, with the pike lying just below the edge of the shelf, at their ambush point.

You will also find pike in the large, shallow expanses of the Broads. Fringed with rushes, they have produced some incredible pike fishing over the years. They are accessible mostly by boat, and can be fished with all sorts of bait and lures. Here you will need to cover a lot of ground before you establish an area where the pike are, unless you are fortunate enough to already know the holding areas.

Locating pike, is for me almost as much fun as catching them. I have had a few good catches over the years, but none are remembered so well as those I made either entirely on my own, perhaps where I had been told there were no fish, or when I caught a single fish under difficult conditions. If you think you know where the pike are, work that area thoroughly, for they may be there but not feeding. Never write-off an area until you have tried it at least three times, and even then under different conditions. Pike are susceptible to weather conditions which govern the movements and activities of the bait fish they hunt. Acquire an understanding of this and you begin to develop that sixth sense that lets you 'know' where the fish are likely to be, and if they will feed.

Pike Care

Pike, because of their fierce appearance and jaw full of teeth, have been the subject of some pretty poor treatment over the years. Pike are not like carp or tench, which survive for some length of time out of water. Unhooking, weighing and photographing should all be done in one swift operation; as one of Britain's leading fish photographers I pride myself on being able to do all three jobs in a little over sixty seconds, though much depends on the hooking of the pike—a deep-hooked pike may take longer.

Aside from grayling, pike have to be the worst candidates for surviving time out of water. One of the reasons is that they can get gassed up with an air bubble inside them, which causes them to drift belly up, even though the gills are still working. The only way round this is to gently stake the fish out in shaded water using a bankstick placed either side to keep it upright. Occasionally you will get a pike that dies for no apparent reason, even when you have followed the correct procedure and handled them as quickly as possible. One of the better ways of dealing with pike is to unhook them first, then put them back in the water in your landing net to regain strength. This is particularly helpful when a fish has fought hard. Then after a few minutes bring them out, weigh and photograph them, then slip them back quickly.

You should not lay your catch on dry gravel or concrete paths. Wet grass is alright, but for unhooking either buy an unhooking mat, or make your own for nothing from a piece of foam rubber with plastic stitched over it. For retaining fish for either a match or photograph, use a large carp sack with extra holes cut in, using one sack for each fish if they are large. A large keepnet, knotless, will also do for a short time, but it is not ideal; you can lose pike from them if the net is left open at the top. I have seen two double-figure fish launch themselves from the keepnet, leaping through the open top like a polaris missile, crashing into the water and swimming away! It makes you jump I can assure you! Everybody should have the option of photographing their catch, so although the use of sacks is not popular with everyone, if rules allow it, and you retain the fish for the minimum period, use one and no harm is done.

The best method of securing a pike for the unhooking procedure is to straddle it. You can feel a bit silly straddling a four pounder—and onlookers might wonder exactly what you are doing—but for fish up to double figures you can use a glove and gently open the jaws by the *front* of the gill cover. On no account touch the gills, which have a toothed edge anyway and will scratch you if the pike suddenly thrashes around. For double-figure pike, straddle them, and gently tilt the head up, following the same procedure. There is

Just look at the power built into the body of this big pike. The photos have already been taken, and the fish is about to be returned.

no need for the pike gag of yesteryear, unless you can modify one to have an adjuster suited to each fish.

The problem with the old spring gags, aside from the forked barbs on the end which are prehistoric, is that the spring has the power of a bear trap and is intended for a forty pounder. Use the same gag on small four pounders and you can rip their jaw hinges. Hopefully some tackle company will come up with an enterprising adjustable gadget that can hold a pike's jaws apart without causing it stress and enable an angler fishing alone to operate with both hands on a deep-hooked pike. I still see problems with many youngsters who, despite the safety of a glove, are frightened of a thrashing pike with those teeth. There is little point in resorting to the barbarism of the old pike gag, but I do see a place for a circular, adjustable tube which slots into a pike's mouth and enables the forceps to be slid down the inside of the tube without damaging fish or fingers. Although I don't use a glove, and use just my fingers for opening the jaws (my experience with the jaws of game fish housing considerably more teeth than the pike's have made me unafraid) a tube-jaw-opening-device would still be great for youngsters or new-comers to the sport.

If the trace disappears down the throat of a pike you may think all is lost—there is no way yet to avoid the occasional deep-hooked pike, unless you use a bait with no hooks—but there are three ways of unhooking to try. If you can pull gently on the wire the stomach lining may invert and the hooks suddenly appear. Don't start yanking on the wire or pulling hard otherwise you will pop the insides and end up with a dead or dying pike. Experience will tell you just how hard you can pull. With a single treble rig, which is mainly what I use, it is easy enough to see the shank of the hook. If it is in the stomach lining you will find there is no way you can turn the hooks upside down to free them from that angle. (Though you could with my idea of a throat-tube gag and angled forceps.) Poke the forceps in through the gill cover, avoiding the gill rakers and you should find a much better grip and angle for turning over, and removing those trebles. You may need two pairs of forceps or an extra pair of hands to prise the gut off each hook. If you use barbless or semi-barbless trebles they will pop out easily.

This is as far as you can safely go down to get your hooks out. If they are this far down, you will do better to approach from the gill opening, avoiding touching the gills, turn the hooks over, and simply pop them out.

An angler returns a good pike that fell to a carp livebait.
Always allow the fish to swim off under its own power. Do
not push it out into the lake.

Above: Night piking is surely for the dedicated. While it doesn't produce large numbers of fish, it does throw up the odd specimen. Here Jerry Airey waits for a run.

Right: Lure collecting can border on obsession. Essex angler Jerry Airey has got the 'lure bug' and now has a collection that leaves him with too many choices. Half a dozen plugs are often enough for a session.

Facing page: While winter is thought of as the traditional time for piking, autumn is possibly more fruitful. This angler fishes a trout livebait near some lilies in the hope of a fish.

The author admires a pair of pike taken on twitched deadbaits. Even a pike of 8lb will put up a good scrap if caught on light spinning tackle.

The author looks delighted with this big double caught at dusk. It took a dead perch he found floating in the margins, and fell to his last cast of the day. Note the light bonefish spinning rod.

Above: Fishery bailiff Mark Simmonds assists with the unhooking of a double-figure pike. Even if you haven't caught the fish, watch to see how deep unhooking is done.

Right: Pike feed almost exclusively on other fish. Years ago it was thought the pike left perch alone because of their spiny dorsal fin. That is untrue, all they do is fold the spiny fin down when they swallow the fish head first. The biggest pike the author has landed on a dead perch weighed 23½lb!

Facing page: This is the author's best catch of pike taken on one of his favourite methods: float-trolling from a boat. There are a few 'doubles' in this lot, with over 100lb for a total weight. All the fish were returned after weighing and photographing.

The Semtex Special! The author hangs on as a Throop fishery river pike explodes across the surface. It was landed on a Ryobi Quivertip rod, the pike taking a lump of cheese the author intended for chub!
Inset: The author with the culprit, a lean river pike.

Pike Care

The problem arises when you use those awful snap tackles with two trebles close together. If both have disappeared down the stomach you may be unable to turn the top treble over as the second is still caught. For trebles that are past access, and to prevent further distress to the fish, use a pair of wire cutters and crush or cut the hooks into pieces. An ordinary pair of wire snips can be extended by sliding some eight inches of tube over the handles. Years ago, and maybe still today, anglers used to cut the wire, rather than the hooks. If you do this, the pike can still survive for a while, but will have what I call "staple-stomach", and be unable to pass large fish down its tract for digestion. It may only feed on fry, in which case it can easily be recognised by its long, lean appearance, but I feel it is worth an extra minute of trying to recover or crunch/cut the hooks rather than leave hooks inside them. Should you use the Patridge VB single hooks the problem is eased, and I advise only one bait-retaining barb on any treble hook. Providing you keep the fish on a tight line it shouldn't drop out. Results from personal tagging done at a variety of venues have seen pike responding better if the barbs were crushed completely.

I should like to see a national tagging programme for pike, the results of which would give us a much clearer indication of the growth and survival of this, our main predator. Of all the pike I tagged, only one four pounder appeared suicidal. In the space of three months I took him from different swims using three different techniques: spinner, deadbait and livebait. I was also surprised to learn just how many pike there are in some waters, and I had a good deal more tags going out, than coming back in the shape of recaptures! It makes for interesting work, and I was using the opercular tagging, promoted about twenty years ago by the specimen groups of the time.

These groups were responsible for the first "PUT PIKE BACK" campaign that aroused interest in promoting this quarry for future sport, rather than slaughtering indiscriminately. Much is owed to them, as they pushed the sport of piking out of the dark ages, with tagging as a means of providing factual information. I am writing this in September 1989, and was surprised to discover that I was using opercular tagging on pike as far back as 22 years ago.

Go Fishing for Pike

An airborne double-figure fish having just been hooked on a carp livebait. Carp are probably the species with the best stamina for piking.

Twenty-two years? It seems like yesterday.

To confirm that the pike does not survive poor handling I can quote Mark Simmonds of Broadlands lake in Hampshire, manager of one of the finest pike fisheries of its size in Britain. With the intense angling pressure the water gets he told me he had to restock every year with pike to maintain a balance that would allow anglers some sport. Although many were lost in spawning, a fact which surely happens in the wild, many were also killed by poor handling.

For myself I like catching any pike, under any conditions, with any technique. If you are just starting out don't aim too high: a ten pounder is still a great fish, and a three or four pounder on light spinning tackle is fun indeed. Respect the pike with careful handling, and he may just surprise you one day when you think that last cast is unlikely to catch anything!

50

Techniques

There are many different fancy end rigs that modern pike anglers can use, but at the end of the day there are still only three basic methods: lure fishing, deadbaiting and livebaiting. Of the three, livebaiting is possibly the easiest, and therefore the most successful, but it is also the most controversial. I have no intention of writing about the latest ultra-cult hooking rig as I do not follow fashions myself. It is better for the beginner to associate himself with these three methods before trying to diversify into something which probably catches more anglers than fish!

Lure Fishing

An artificial lure is something that should represent food to the pike, causing it to strike and hopefully hook up. However, the second a pike grabs a lure he realises the metal or plastic object is not edible and will try to eject it fast. In the same split second the pike thinks this, you should react even faster and strike, thereby setting the hooks. Lure fishing is very pleasant as you need the minimum of tackle, are mobile, and can use only one rod at a time. Therefore you need to be constantly aware of what is going on at the lure end of things, and vary your retrieve to imitate a healthy, wounded or dying fish depending on the action of your lure.

There are now more lures available to the angler than ever before due to the importation of many American plugs marketed for striped and largemouth black bass. The range is almost limitless,

Go Fishing for Pike

Sporting a treble hook in front and rear, the "Professor" spoons are excellent for a wide range of pike. Note the bead 'eye', which the author thinks makes them successful, after reaching a similar conclusion using "eyed" deadbaits.

and collectors are held in great esteem if they have a couple of unusual or rare discontinued models in their collection. If you find trouble purchasing lures from the American freshwater fishing magazines, there are one or two importers that ship them in. As with anything imported, they are likely to be much more expensive that those you can buy in America. Artificial lures are something of a misnomer. You can have an artificial bait, but not surely an artificial lure! For the purpose of this book I shall call them simply lures.

Now while I have said that lure fishing is a mobile method of fishing, it must be said that the warmer the water temperature the higher your chances of success. It is all to do with metabolism. You are more likely to go rushing around chasing a football on a warm day, than you are in a blizzard in mid-January. Much the same goes for pike. In the cold water of winter they are more likely to lie in ambush making one effort to grab a fish that swims near them, thus conserving energy, than in any of the other three seasons when they are more likely to be on the prowl, slowly finning around on the lookout for baitfish. It is in the warmer weather that they will actively chase a lure, so expect the best of the lure fishing then.

Techniques

Having said that I still fire out a few plugs and spoons during winter, mainly because I enjoy using lures, but also because there are obviously going to be times when your lure passes the nose of a pike in winter and he will grab it. Another point worth noting is that you never seem to get a lot of big pike on lures. I use lures quite a bit, but considering the time put in at the water I would have to say a double-figure fish is something of a rarity, to be cherished and admired, with a twenty pounder as outstanding. I have only had one 20-lb-plus pike on a lure, and I confess that was about as exciting as I want my lure fishing to get.

The story surrounding its capture bears recounting, and if it hadn't happened to me personally I would have stored it in the fiction section! You may be aware that I am reasonably dedicated to fishing. Today I fish less hours for more fish simply because of the experience I have accumulated, but years ago, like so many anglers, I caught my fish by putting in the rod hours. It has been a tradition of mine (until wife number 2), to go fishing on Christmas morning. That day to me was the best fishing day of the year. On Christmas morning it is so quiet you could think the world has ended: there are no jets, no trains, no cars; it is almost eerie. I used to get up at dawn, load the car in the half light and drive the deserted streets where even the milkmen were absent. On this particular morning I had been read the riot act to return at the latest, by 12 noon. I had no baits, just a pocketful of plugs and an old glass carp rod. The venue was one of the gravel pits near my home.

I had been watching the mild drizzly weather stay constant and I knew which end of the lake I wanted to go. When I arrived there only a few coots scattered in alarm and the car park was totally empty, something you wouldn't normally see at this venue unless the four-minute warning had been given.

I had a long walk down to the swim, but when I arrived I stood for a second surveying the water. Tight to some bushes there was a scattering of silver fry, followed by a big swirl. The pike were there. I covered the area for half an hour going through every plug and spinner I had in my pockets. Oh for a wriggling little gudgeon that would scarcely have hit the water before being engulfed. The pike

Go Fishing for Pike

were obviously preoccupied with the fry and wanted nothing of my lure.

Frustrated, I cast farther and farther to the other bank, aiming for a spot where a tree had dipped its roots in the water, a classic place for a pike. Unfortunately it was also a classic place to lose a good lure and my enthusiastic cast sent the lure into the branches. Gentle tweaking failing to produce the required result, and my temper worsening, I pulled it savagely. I guess we have all been in the same situation. Then just when I thought I might uproot the tree entirely, my rod split and I was left gaping at a stump about three feet long, with the other end sliding gracefully under the surface. I'd had that rod a dozen years and taken no end of good barbel, carp and pike on it. I tightened on the line and walked backward hoping the broken half would slide back towards me. No chance. The line broke and it dropped into ten feet of water!

A splash to my left indicated there was still a pike boiling after the fry by the overhanging bushes. Right! That was it! I determined to catch a pike of any size on what remained of my gnome-like rod, even if I had to get in there and kick it out. I pushed in between the bushes to where an outflow stream flowed and found I could now make an angled cast to my left through a gap in the bushes, which was actually made easier by having just three feet of rod. The first two casts yielded nothing, so I changed to an American silver plug called a "Big O". The cast was perfect and I started the retrieve. When it neared the bushes it stopped dead and I pulled back thinking I had snagged an underwater root or branch. The snag pulled back. In fact I was forced to backwind so fast I rapped my knuckles.

It took me five or ten minutes to subdue that fish as its size became painfully apparent . . . it was large! I glanced round for my net . . . yes, I had forgotten it, and had left it in the car. My only option, there not being another angler in sight, was to try and beach it up the outflow ditch. As the pike thrashed around I eased the drag and using just finger pressure on the spool used my three-foot rod to steer it up the ditch where I dropped on it, grappling with it in the shallow water like I was panning for gold. I knew it was a big double, but just how big?

Techniques

What a Christmas Day present! The author's smile says it all as he cradles a beautifully-marked 20-lb-plus pike, his largest taken on a lure.

I reasoned the only thing to do was make a stringer out of my reel line and stake it out in the water. I used several yards of my 12-lb line, threaded it through the bottom jaw, pushed the big pike into the deep water and tied the other end round a tree root. I knew from experience the fish would lie still if kept dark, so quietly I laid some grass and leaves over its head and shortened my leash until it was a foot from the bank.

If the fish lunged it would cut the line and swim away unhindered, but I now had to find a witness. Who could I call on Christmas Day? Adrian Hutchins was my first choice, mainly because he would be the only one who might give credence to my story. As I raced back home I thought about how I was going to explain things if we arrived back to find just a length of nylon. It was a gamble, but a worthwhile one. It took five minutes to convince his family that he wouldn't be late for Christmas lunch (I knew he would be, so did he!), and with cameras and scales roared back to the lake. It probably took an hour all round. Exhausted, I waded out and slid my hand down the length of nylon, dreading I would find the chafed ends. But no — they stopped with a bump on the pike's jaws and I gently eased round behind it to lift it from the water. Adrian slid the net under and I was once again the proud captor of a pike. It kicked the Avons past the 20-lb mark and I set it up for the photographs. As the fish was eased back into the water, I realised it was possibly the best Christmas present I had ever had. I mean you just don't get 20-lb plus pike wrapped up in paper under the Christmas tree do you?

That little story illustrates my most exciting catch with lures. Lures can be sub-divided into four categories: floating plugs, sinking plugs, spinners and wobblers. I have always had a lot of success using plugs, but then they spend a long time in the water, whereas spinners and wobblers get used less frequently. The best of the floating plugs come from the States where they have devised dozens of models for surface fishing the black bass. I would venture to suggest that they are an audible, rather than visual attractor, as they incorporate a scoop or bucket shape on the front to trap air.

Basically you cast out towards some weedbeds like lilies, let the plug settle after hitting the surface, then with a sharp flick of the wrist impart some action via the rod top to jerk the plug forwards a foot or so. This traps air in the front cup which causes an audible bloop. Instead of retrieving you simply let the plug just sit there, for as long as two minutes. The theory is that Mr Bass comes out of his snaggy hole to investigate the cause of this bloop, so when you bloop it the second time, he dives for it. Our own pike responds to these lures as well, they are known as "popping" plugs because of the sound they emit, but I have yet to catch a pike after leaving the plug static and soundless for as long as two minutes. Certainly the pike are attracted to this popping sound, but the success of the plugs appears to be limited to shallow water, especially around weedbeds which is where the fish are going to hang out anyway. I hold the theory that perhaps audible sounds carry farther through shallow water than deep, though it is only a theory.

I have also found I enjoy success most in the stillwaters of estate lakes which are also basically shallow, the edges of a slow-moving canal or lock outflows on rivers, but much depends on the weed-beds of the area. My own opinion on surface popping plugs is that they are ideal for the fisherman who wants to break the monotony of a few blanks, where a change is as good as a rest.

You can also purchase surface plugs that are not popping, but create turbulence by two small propellors front and aft. I have taken a couple of pike on these but generally use them for striped bass; they can be retrieved at a constant rate. Pencil plugs are another type of surface lure. Long and thin like a pencil, they are retrieved quite fast through the surface film, and may be a useful addition to the arsenal primarily in summertime when the water is warm.

More conventional for the British pike angler is the sub-surface plug. If you are a beginner and you just walk into your local tackle shop and ask for a floating plug you could encounter some problems. There are many makes of plugs that float, but they may

In the still Irish mist the author steers a big pike towards his landing net. Always keep the rim on the net submerged and slide the pike over it quietly.

not necessarily be popping plugs. If they have a sloping chin or vane at the front they will dive to varying degrees beneath the water surface. When not retrieved they will float! Hence a second type of floating plug.

In America such lures are called "Crankbaits". You throw them out and crank them back! These lures are the mainstay of my fishing, and believe me, you can spend a small fortune on all the different types available. Some are gimmicks, some don't even work properly, and a few are very good indeed. Having tried most of them I have now discarded all except two types. The first is the balloon-shaped alphabet plug like the Ryobi "Mugger", Shakespeare "Big S", or the Heddon range, all of which are very good. They can be fitted with heavier gauge treble hooks, and the barbs of each treble can be partially crushed with pliers to make them semi-barbless. A plug is only grabbed by predators, not turned and swallowed, so there are no problems with deep hooking.

With the second type of plug, the Abu Hi-Lo plug, you have an adjustable vane on the front to alter the depth at which it can be fished, plus a different rate of retrieves with which to alter the action. The Hi-Lo is jointed, as opposed to the aforementioned three plugs which are all single. If I had a favourite to fish with, it would be the "Big S" in the rusty brown colour. I have caught a huge number of pike on it, including some double-figure fish. The beauty of the floating plug is that you can wind it back slowly, just over the tops of weedbeds or snags, then make it dive deeper by winding faster. When cranked back hard they dive several feet deep and set a thick, vibrant action. The Americans usually fish them by working their boats around the edges of deep lakes. The margin shelves away slowly for about two feet, then drops suddenly. The predators work along this shelf, and seldom hit a plug when it is out in the deep clear water. In tournaments the American angler will cast to the bank, engage the reel then crank the plug fast through this shelf area where the fish are most likely to be. The more times they can pull the lure through this shelf area, the greater the chance of it being taken, and maybe winning the tournament. This is called "Kill Zone" fishing.

In the U.K. kill zone fishing may work on occasions where the

Techniques

RYOBI market the successful "Mugger" artificial lures. Upgrade the trebles to something heavier as these plugs can often entice big pike.

pike are known to be holding at a certain depth, but if you have to search around, the "Big S" and similar plugs like the Ryobi "Mugger" will allow you to cover varying depths by altering your speed of retrieve. You can even 'crawl' them over 6 inches of water where jack pike will hammer them and make you jump three feet, especially when they hit just as you are about to take the plug from the water.

Jointed plugs like the Abu Hi-Lo tend to have faster retrieve patterns, and whereas the single plugs have their own vibrant action under a steady retrieve, the jointed plugs may need some assistance to make them lifelike. You can inject life in them by jerking the rod top every turn or two of the reel handle. The best way to do this is to watch the plug in clear, shallow water, and when you have the action you require, remember it and duplicate it for future casts.

A small point worth remembering is to do with reels. You now have the excellent Aero range of fixed spools on the market by

Shimano. They have the spool capacity to fire your lure out to new horizons, which is great as you will be covering more water. But you have to remember the elastic properties of a long length of monofilament fishing line. At long distance it will largely absorb the action you intend imparting to the lure via your rod tip. Therefore on a long cast be sure to exaggerate the action on the rod top, to hopefully relay it down the line to the lure. The alternative is to use a non-stretch or pre-stretched nylon line, but problems are encountered when setting the hooks on a pike that hits at close range. Ordinary mono can absorb that shock, but pre-stretched has a tendency to snap under shock. I think it best to stick with ordinary mono and just exaggerate your tip action on the rod for the first one third of the retrieve.

Occasionally I have found pike falling to a fast "crank" retrieve, but most of the time a steady retrieve provokes most response. Certainly there are a couple of points worth considering for sub-surface plug fishing. Do you want your lure to imitate a dead or dying fish, or one that is healthy, and thereby trying to escape from its hunter? My own method of retrieve is to imitate the sort of speed you would expect a normal healthy fish to adopt: a steady few turns of the handle to cover several feet, followed by a hard jerk on the tip to impart a darting action to the lure, perhaps suggesting to the pike a fish trying to escape. I try to cover as much of the area in front of me as possible with this speed of retrieve, and that goes for pretty nearly all the sub-surface plugs I use, regardless of action. If I still have the 'hots' for that swim, and I'm certain there is a pike at home, I take more care with a much slower retrieve, and impart more jerks on the rod top to impart violent darts at short intervals to the lure. Always make sure you watch for the shape of the lure before you lift off for the next cast. You will be surprised at the number of pike that follow a slow, erratic lure right in to the bank. The faster retrieve generally creates a more violent take, so be prepared for even a small bump on the line or rod tip, indicating a fish has hit the lure. You need to wind and strike. Don't wait any longer than necessary to sink the hooks.

Another tip worth remembering when lure fishing is that the pike is liable to be hooked on the rear set of trebles. Because many plugs

Techniques

The author's camera captures the power on this big Irish pike which has already left the water in the foreground of the picture, and is currently on its second leap skywards. Now is the time you don't set your reel clutch.

sport at least two sets of trebles, that leaves a spare set to get tangled in the mesh of the net. It has happened to me dozens of times, so remember if you net a fish and can see the plug is hanging from the side of the jaws, net it, but get straight on top of it once it's on the bank to prevent it flailing around. One set of trebles will probably get snagged in the mesh anyway, and small pike under 8lb or so have a tendency to roll themselves up in the mesh. This snags the trebles further, and results in the fish being out of the water an excessively long time. Also you may have to cut the mesh to get the trebles out. If you grab the fish straight away you prevent this.

Alternatively use a thick leather glove and lift it out by putting your thumb in the bottom jaw. This is what Americans call the

If the hook is well down, go carefully in through the gill cover, taking care not to damage the gill rakers, and this will allow you to turn the treble or single hook over and pop it free. Once free, you can use the full length of the artery forceps to poke the hook free from the jaws. This pike is NOT being held by the gill rakers, but by the main hinge of the lower jaw where a) the angler avoids getting cut by teeth, and b) the fingers don't even touch the delicate gill rakers. Some anglers like to use gloves, but once confidence has been attained by experience, a glove is not required. Big pike can be laid on an unhooking mat, and straddled by the angler to prevent them thrashing around.

'lip-lift' and they use it on bass. It's fine on small jacks but no good on bigger fish. Pike to about 6lb can be lifted out by grabbing them behind the head with your free hand—the opercular flaps stop them sliding off. This is the method I favour most when wading, and is only a method to get them to the bank where proper unhooking can be done. If the pike is only hooked in the scissors you can unhook them while still wading then slip them straight back. As mentioned before, speed is of the essence when dealing with this species.

For boat fishing you can obviously anchor or drift and cast out any type of plug. This is a particularly good method on small lakes where you can easily cover the water by drifting. But the bigger single-bodied plugs that you can buy are more suited to trolling from a moving boat than casting and retrieving. Use either the power of the outboard to run the boat, or oars. The old Seagull outboards, although dated, are trusty machines and ideally suited for trolling. I prefer them to the modern outboards. On large deep waters you need to run them so the plug is pulling quite hard, and the action accentuated to a fine hum. This gives a good vibration factor, and also makes for a hell of a violent take when the pike hits the lure. If you use the oars however, you will be going that much slower and the pike will have a split-second chance to throw the plug. Rather than use those rod clamps that bolt to the side of the boat, I prefer to troll with just two rods, one leaning out at 45 degrees from each corner, and I put my foot on the butt of the rods, as I row along. That way, as soon as I see a fish hit I can ship the oars, reach down, grab the rod in question and set the hook immediately; it also gives the fish less time to throw those hooks. The bigger lochs and lakes that lend themselves to this style of plug trolling also give me the best response with the bigger plugs. Naturally it doesn't always get the biggest fish, but at least I'm catching something!

Moving on from plugs you have spinners and spoons. Again the tackle shops are fairly well supplied with the different models available, although pike anglers seem to collect plugs rather than spinners. A spinner can better be described as a bar-like spoon. That is, a piece of polished metal that revolves, or spins around a stem of wire with a swivel at one end, and a treble at the other. As for movement in the water, the revolving blade is constant in action, varying only in the speed of your retrieve. If you wind extremely fast they simply cannot bite water and pop up from the surface.

My own preference when using this lure is to wind as slowly as possible without the spinner hitting bottom, but making sure there is a constant throbbing on the rod tip from the revolving blade. Also remember that the larger the blade, the slower it will revolve for a given speed. Small spinners are fast, big spinners slow. My best and most successful spinner for pike was a Veltic Red on sliver number four. They also made a green, but this size in the red was a fantastic pike catcher. For smaller bladed spinners you have the Mepps range. Primarily a game fish lure, it too accounts for a large number of pike. As a general rule I have found smaller fish hit more spinners than plugs, and I have only taken a few doubles on revolving blade spinners.

In contrast are spoons, which are curved pieces of shiny metal that wobble and flutter their way through the water rather than spin. They certainly account for larger pike, possible because they are larger in size and therefore reflect a larger amount of light and flash. They are also very good when trolled either from a powered or rowed boat. A point worth noting is that a heavy-gauge metal spoon might cast well, but you will not be able to fish it slowly in shallow to medium depth water. Keep the "heavy metals" for deep-water boat trolling, and for shallower water opt for thin spoons that have a large surface area and can be made to flutter. I have no idea if other lure enthusiasts have the same success rate with thin, large-area spoons as I normally fish alone, but they certainly might help you pick off a few extra pike.

Smaller spoons like the Odin range from Ryobi Masterline or the Abu Toby are good mainly for jack pike. Select the lighter range for the reasons stated before, and retrieve with an occasional flick of the rod top to make the lure give off that extra flash of light. The large area spoons will flash well anyway, but in coloured water particularly, it doesn't hurt to give the rod a flick and make that flashing movement a bit brighter. Finally there is something called a Spinnerbait that is all the rage at present. While Spinnerbaits may be new for the British angler they have been used for decades in

The author returns a 14lb 6 oz pike to an Irish lake. He believes that Ireland is one of the last few places where a "natural"

Above: This pike fell to a live carp fished near the margins of a reedbed. Never neglect the water directly in front of you, as pike will use any margins as cover from which to ambush their prey.

Left: The mounted head of this 21-lb Scottish pike has one of the most popular shaped lures in its jaws. If livebaiting is outlawed, anglers will have to learn more about the art of using artificial lures for this species.

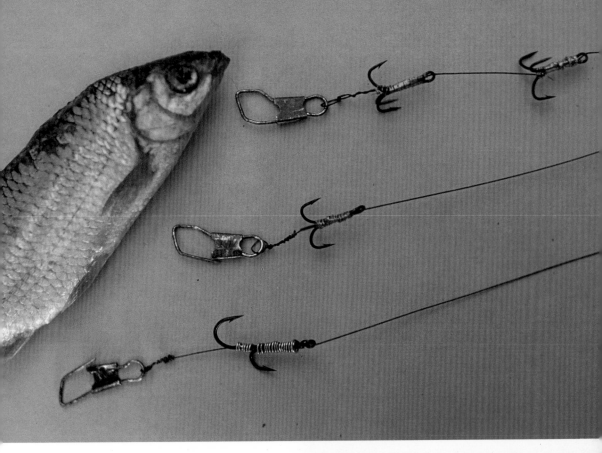

Above: The author's invention of the 'Lip-Clip' for use in twitched deadbaits or livebaiting. An American snap-swivel has been cut down to leave just the clip/loop, which has been widened to fit the top lip of any baits. The hooks are whipped tight to the wire trace by copper wire. Top row: instant strike rig. Centre: Single treble Partridge. Bottom: Partridge VB single hook for weedy conditions.

Right: Large spoons are particularly effective when fished from a boat in deep water or trolled under power. These two are marketed by Ryobi.

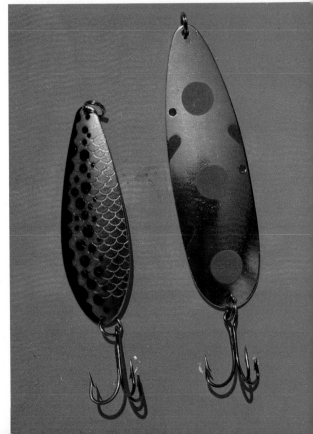

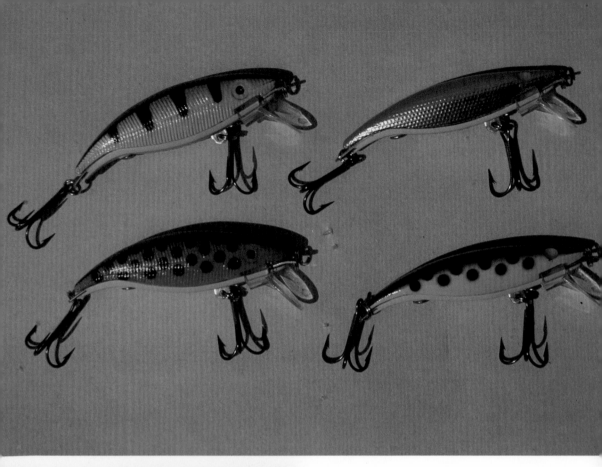

Above: A selection of plugs from the Ryobi stable.

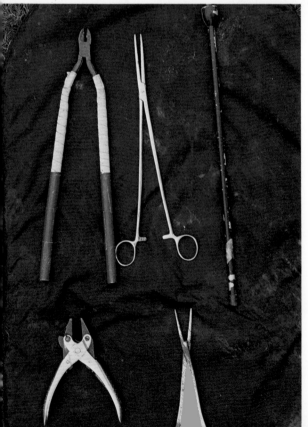

Left: These are the essentials for extracting hooks. On the right, the deep throat disgorger extracts single trebles that may have slipped out of sight in the stomach lining. Centre is a pair of extra-long forceps. Top left shows a pair of wire cutters fitted with extension handles—these are used for cutting up hooks that cannot be removed. Bottom right shows a standard pair of forceps, and bottom left, a pair of pliers with sidecutters for extracting hooks from landing net mesh!

Above: Pike fishing has its share of legends. This is the legend of Dogmersfield lake, found when the author was head bailiff there. This skull illustrates perfectly the teeth layout of the pike.

Right: The Ryobi spinnerbaits. Used primarily in the American largemouth bass waters, this lure is getting more popular with British pike anglers. They look odd, but they catch fish.

Paul Harris with four pike landed by the author on a trip to the River Shannon. Paul was fishing the pole for roach, and was constantly pestered by pike, which delighted the author as he was given the job of extracting them. Twitched dead roach did the business.

Pike don't eat tench? Paul Harris can testify that this is wrong, as this 17- lb fish tried to eat a 3-lb tench he was playing. Paul removed the offending pike with a deadbait, then continued to net 50lb of tench!

Micky Hills from Chandler's Ford took these four doubles on a floatfished trout livebait. The venue was Broadlands lake in Hampshire.

America, mostly for the large and smallmouth bass. I have caught bass on them for years, though even to this day I cannot see why fish take them! They look like a spinner which has been extended to look like a bent coathanger with a lead and shredded plastic hanging from it. They look ridiculous, but they certainly have a mesmeric effect on predators. In contrast to plugs and spoons they fish best if you retrieve them at a constant rate, as smoothly and evenly as possible. When largemouth bass fishing, the rod is held high, the tip pointed at 45 degrees and the spinnerbait retrieved in short wrist jerks that presumably make the plastic strips flutter. For pike I have found the constant retrieve to be the most successful, but do try the bass method as well, particularly when working near lilies and surface weedbeds.

This, then is a brief insight into the use of lures in pike fishing. It is an entertaining way to fish and pleasurable in that you don't have mammoth tackle boxes to drag around: a rod, reel, landing net, lures and unhooking implements are all you need. The growth of lure fishing in Britain has been considerable. Now there is renewed enthusiasm with pikers trying new lures, rods and reels to get more satisfaction from their sport. While fishing with lures may not be as successful across the board as livebaiting, a pike taken on a lure does give you that feeling that you really deserve that fish for fooling it into hitting a piece of plastic or wood!

Livebaiting

Now here is a topical point if ever there was one. Livebaiting has been likened to the tethering of a goat to entice a tiger to kill. I can see the comparison from a non-anglers point of view, because the 'tethering' of the fish reduces its chances of escape, whereas in the wild predators chase their live prey naturally. I think in the future livebaiting probably will be banned. But that won't stop pike eating other fish so I cannot really see the point. My argument, if I need one, is that by using a single baitfish to catch a pike, the subsequent capture and resultant stress on the pike will prevent it feeding again in a hurry, and thereby allow a few more baitfish to swim un-harmed. A conservationist's own goal I call it!

Go Fishing for Pike

These livebaits have been stored in a specially constructed tank at the pike water. If there is a syndicate pike water, this would be an excellent way to store livebait ready for use.

While I have no qualms about livebaiting with small, immature or stunted fish, I have my own hypocritical moral grounds for not using any livebait that is over half a pound in weight. While a few dead fish aren't going to keep me awake at night it is the fact that many youngsters or beginners would be pleased to catch a fish of that weight, that stops me using them. I've seen a 12-oz dace, a 1¼-lb roach, a 2-lb chub and a 1-lb rudd all used as livebait at one time or another. Baits of 3 to 6 ounces are fine, and are so abundant they are unlikely to be missed while the use of over sized baits can surely only lend ammunition to the anti-anglers. I also appreciate that there can be little difference in the tethering of a 2-oz gudgeon or a 2-lb chub — both are likely to be eaten by a predator — but we all had low target weights for species as youngsters, so let's leave them with something worth catching.

Techniques

Having said all that I have to admit that livebaiting must surely be the most successful method for pike fishing. It is also the easiest, because there is no way an angler can simulate a live fish by lure fishing or twitching a deadbait. A fish swimming through the water has a snake-like side-to-side wiggle. There isn't a lure on the market that can do that, nor can a lure swim vertically towards the surface while fluttering on its side while trying to escape a pike! The closest action I have seen to that is the sea fishing lure called a Redgill sandeel. That its tail has a very fishy wiggle must surely be why it is the most successful sea angling lure ever devised.

You can anchor, floatfish or freeline a livebait, and basically it is going to swim where it wants. You can restrict that area a little, but the beauty of livebait fishing is that you can cover water. You can also have a moving and vibrating bait in one confined area which other methods cannot give. Livebaiting must be the greatest short-cut to success in pike fishing, and it is particularly suited to beginners who have little knowledge of tackle and techniques. Newcomers can throw out a livebait under a float and have every confidence that it will be taken, and learn about the refinements that can be made to the terminal rig later.

Now comes the problem — the acquisition of baits! In mid-winter when pike are less likely to chase a lure, bait fishing can be very successful. Unfortunately winter means cold weather, which means catching bait is difficult. My tip is to fish slow-moving rivers and streams avoiding stillwaters unless they are known to be productive. You also have to be aware that most clubs and water authorities have restrictions on fish movements. Please check your rule book or with your water authority before catching fish and transporting them or you could find yourself in trouble. The rules are there to minimise any spread of fish disease, and any movements of fish usually require the relevant paperwork to be filled out. That pike anglers catch fish in one place to use them in another is well known, and the way to get round this is to buy in baits from an authorised dealer. He should have a clean bill of health for all his stock, which means they shouldn't carry any disease.

If you think that is an expensive way to go about acquiring bait think again. You have maggots to buy, maybe groundbait. You have to spend a minimum of half a day at the water, time that could be spent pike fishing. You need food and drink, petrol to travel to the venue, and then, if you are following the rules, you have to fish that bait at the same water, which may not be a good pike water. Its sod's law that if you go to a good pike water you will never catch a bait there, so you can see why it might pay you to buy your livebaits from a professional fish farmer.

Having bought some bait you will want to keep them alive. This can be done initially by transporting them in a bucket or mini bin with a plastic lid and aeration pump fitted. Just cut a hole in the top of the lid to slide in the tube and aeration stone, and cut a slot in the edge of the lid to hang the aeration unit on. This avoids water slopping onto the car floor which leads to unseen rust. We used to joke that if you bought a second-hand car you looked under the mat to see if rust spots were there. If you found some, the chances were that the owner was an illegal livebaiter. Something like the old liquor runners in the prohibition days of America!

When you get the baits home you can store them in a large plastic dustbin, keeping them either in the garage, or outside. If you put them outside, make sure they are under an overhang or roof to minimise the chances of their freezing in cold weather. Some of the more eccentric livebaiters have special storage tanks at the back of their gardens to house the different size fish. I find a large dustbin is sufficient and in cold weather there is enough oxygen in the water to take about forty small fish. The exception to this is the storage of trout: they need an intensive oxygen supply and an aeration unit running all the time. I now use a large aquarium with a commercial aeration unit when I intend to do some serious sessions on pike. Livebaits will live for weeks without food, presumably using their body fats stored up from the autumn, but in warm weather they will start to die if you don't feed them. If the water temperature gets too hot, you should tip some out, and refill under pressure from a hose. This pumps oxygen in and cools the temperature. Remove any dead fish immediately and freeze them down for deadbaits.

When it comes to the transportation of baits from tank to venue, use the same bucket with its plastic lid, but make a scoop from plastic mesh so you can get your baits out without dipping your hand in freezing water. You can buy a small dip net at aquarium shops, but a good tip is to bind it to some coathanger wire to stiffen it. When the baits are in, fill the bucket to the top, put on the lid, and press a piece of foam rubber into the hole around the aeration tube. This prevents water slopping over the carpet of the car.

On arrival, as well as using portable battery pumps, some pike anglers have rigged up a pump with an extension lead to run from the cigarette lighter of the car. This saves on portable battery units which can then be used to get the baits down to the bank or boat. After that you will either need to keep feeding batteries into the pump if you run it all day, or you can put it on for fifteen minute periods then switch it off. You could also take a small cut-down keepnet to put the baits in the water, especially if you are staying in one swim. Or you can take the foam and aerator off the bucket drain out the water and refill it with fresh water about every hour. In hot weather I have heard of anglers dropping those blue freezer blocks into the bucket to keep the temperature low and the oxygen high. As you can see the intricacies of livebaiting are far more

"The author uses long-nosed artery forceps to extract the hook from this double figure Loch Muckno pike. He rarely uses more than one treble hook, and hopes to hook most of the pike in the scissors. Barbless hooks aid unhooking."

difficult and time consuming than just throwing the fish into the water with a hook in them!

Two final tips on those buckets. The best ones come through the building trade, but make sure they are completely cleaned of their contents. I once heard of an angler using a plastic bucket that previously housed the paint for junior's bedroom. When he took out the first bait in the half light of dawn both his hand and the bait were pink! The second tip is to make a wire frame or plastic mesh inner liner for the bucket like those deep fat friers. This allows you to lift all the baits out and make a selection, rather than leaving you to rummage around for a supercharged gudgeon until your fingers, and the air, turns blue.

Having given you some idea about how to go about collecting and storing livebait we should now look at which baits catch pike. For pike baits read anything that swims! Any species, including tench are taken by pike, although some species come higher on their list than others. Years ago in the old books the tench was called the Doctor fish. The slime covering this species was reputed to have

This angler has a meshed liner to his livebait container for avoiding freezing hands when he wants another bait.

healing properties so powerful that other species rubbed up against their flanks to be cured. Even the pike was supposed to have this reverence for the tench. Let me assure you (though I believed it all as a youngster), a pike isn't going to be sidling up against the flank of any tench. If the pangs of hunger are strong the only time a pike touches a tench's flank is when the latter is disappearing down its gullet! I bet with all that slime the tench slide down well too.

The reasons I believe tench do not get taken too often by pike are firstly because they are well camouflaged against the bottom. Secondly they are more active at night, when the pike is quieter, and thirdly because the average British tench is probably 2lb or so. Quite a bite for the average 8-lb pike. I have never used a tench for livebait purely because I could never catch them small enough to put on a hook. However, the fact that pike eat tench was highlighted to me when I was in Ireland a year or so back. I was fishing a lake with Paul Harris of the Irish Tourist Board and some other lads. Paul was fishing a feeder for tench, and hammering them too. I think he finished with over 50lb. One of the tench, about 3lb was fighting close to the bank when this huge pike struck and thrashed about in an effort to take the tench. Suffice to say Mr. Tench was landed, but Mr. Perch soon found himself airborne in the direction of Mr. Pike! Poor chap, he was demolished immediately and the pike landed at 17lb, the same fish that had tried to take Paul's tench.

I find that for a flashy bait to attract a pike you cannot beat a small dace. They keep fairly well in cold weather and are first-class baits in both coloured and clear water. I rate them highly. In coloured or peaty water I find both perch and rudd are good livebaits. Another fallacy from the pike anglers of the past was that perch never got taken by a pike due to the former having a spiny dorsal fin that caused the pike to choke. Nonsense! They had obviously never fished perch as baits before, because pike have no trouble crunching and collapsing that spiny fin and posting the whole fish to the stomach department. Perch are great baits and last well.

Rudd are less silvery than dace but with their golden sheen and red-tinged fins, they really turn the pike on. They are surprisingly durable and keep well. Roach may be the most popular bait among beginners, mainly because that may be the first baitfish they acquire. On some waters where there is a heavy population of roach the pike become preoccupied with the same species and size of fish, ignoring other offerings. This is particularly so in early winter when they have been hammering roach fry. Roach don't keep too well however, and certainly don't appreciate repeated casting. I would say a couple of casts and they have had it. Consign them to the deadbait freezer.

Top of the list come trout, gudgeon and carp. I have purposely ignored chub because I like catching them, but they are very good baits in the 6–8 ounce range. I refuse to use them in larger sizes. Trout can easily be obtained from any of the fish farmers, but remember they need cool temperatures and lots of oxygen. They do not like repeated casting but chug around very well if you make your first cast count, and then leave it there. You may need to use some sort of restraint like a float-paternoster rig to prevent them charging into the nearest snag or weedbed. If you keep them yourself, a tip from me is to paint the outside of a glass aquarium white as the trout will alter its body colour slightly to blend with the background. Ordinarily they will be quite dark, but they are strong and obviously attract the pike with their vibrations. I first realised you could make your livebaits lighter when I was doing some groundwork for one of my trout books. I was at Bridge Farm with the owner at that time, Phil Herring (his real name). Phil had split some Browns off from the main stews into a clean gravel bottom to lift their colour from a drab brown-gold, to the bronze sheen with bright dot markings of the wildie. I tried it with my pike baits and found it worked, so I pass the tip on to you as I doubt you will find it anywhere else.

Crucian carp are probably the strongest "in" bait among serious pike livebaiters. They are gold in colour and must have copper-coloured batteries fitted as they chug around all day. They are probably the most durable bait I have found. They keep well under a variety of conditions, need less oxygen than other species and tolerate warm water. I was introduced to carp livebaits only recently. This was down at Broadlands where a delivery of 1500 had

Techniques

A superb action shot of an airborne Irish pike. There is little doubt that the Irish fish fight harder than their English counterparts.

arrived for the start of the pike season. They were tiny baits of about four or five inches and had come from a commercial farm. They lasted for as long as it took to get eaten or cast off, and looked really pretty, just like the miniature mirrors and commons. They were possibly the strongest bait I have ever used, and thereby possibly the best pike bait of all.

Finally there is the gudgeon: a small river fish of a couple of ounces that is strong, and constantly works through any depth of water. I use them whenever I can. They survive well in cold weather and even though somewhat drab in appearance can be made to lighten their colouring if kept in a white bucket. They work particularly well in water that is just off-clear. I had better mention bleak and minnows as both are good for small to medium-sized pike. Many years ago the Thames was stiff with bleak and you could get all the baits you needed in an hour. Now they seem to have almost disappeared, but they are silver sided jewels of baits that are great

73

for depths up to six feet. They do not keep well, or take kindly to being cast out repeatedly but are a good bait if you can get enough of them.

Minnows are easy to catch and prolific enough for even young-sters to catch. They are especially good when the pike are feeding on fry near snags or bushes, when they fish best either freelined, or under a 3-swan shot float hooked on a big single hook. They allow for instant striking as soon as the pike has taken the bait.

This should give you enough idea of the best livebaits for pike, for although becoming a controversial method, it is still the easiest way to catch good pike. In a way livebaiting is the shortcut to success.

While all the aforementioned will catch pike at one time or another I feel it worth noting the different depths each species works best at. If pike are on fry, but swirling just below the surface making that tell-tale boil as they grab a fish, you will find that minnows, roach and trout will be the most successful bait. If the pike are actually striking on the surface, or are sending up splinters of scattering fry you need a bait that tries to work near the surface. For this the bleak is best, closely followed by the rudd. Both are natural surface feeders and will therefore be happiest there . . . until a pike comes along! For water of four feet to fifteen feet, or when the pike are not hard on the feed and you need to get a bait down to them, try perch, carp, crucians and gudgeon. They all pull naturally downwards, which makes them move in the area the pike are lying. There would be little point in floatfishing a surface swimming livebait in very cold weather when the pike are semi-dormant on the bottom of the lake. You want a bait that gets alarmed and chugs around close to the bottom.

This should also give you something of a pointer as to the seasons in which to use the different livebaits. Minnows and bleak should be used from autumn to early winter, use perch, trout and roach at the backend of the season after a thaw, and carp, crucians, gudgeon and perch in the cold weather when you need a bait working near the bottom. As you should now see, there is more to livebaiting than just throwing any live fish out. You may catch a pike, but an experienced pike fisherman will catch more, over a longer period.

Techniques

An angler casts out a floatfished deadbait. On large waters it is possible to drift baits out over 100 yards using a vaned pike float.

Deadbaiting

While livebaiting has some controversy surrounding it, the way lies open for the progression of deadbaiting techniques. Some of the biggest pike every year fall to dead fish legered on the bottom, and although seemingly a boring method of fishing when compared to the roving techniques of lures and livebait, it catches fish. When I did my tagging programme I kept a list of fish caught on different baits. Strangely enough it worked out around 50:50, and certainly the larger fish fell to deadbaits.

I think it is useful to have some ideas of techniques and baits, especially when the pike get hammered on livebaits earlier in the season. I feel they skulk around the bottom, and in cold weather particularly may be more inclined to pick up a deadbait. I have climbed trees and watched pike several times investigating a deadbait. Initially they move in to an area after the splash of the bait hitting the surface. Of course some will swim up, engulf the lot and

Pike eat almost anything, as this crayfish can testify. The pike fell to a rudd deadbait, but coughed up this large crayfish on being unhooked.

76

march off, but more often than not they will lie just a few inches, maybe a foot or so, off the bottom just looking at the deadbait. Then something makes them grab it crosswise and they move off, turning it in their jaws. I also found that you could induce a take by tweaking the bait a foot or so.

The best of the natural deadbaits would now be silver, as the natural camouflage of some livebaits make them blend in too well with the mud or debris on the bottom. Remember that while you have the two factors of vibration and flash from livebaits tethered off the bottom, you only have a visual one when you fish a deadbait. It is therefore in your own interest to select a bright bait.

Dace would come top of my list, followed by roach, bleak and rudd. After that I would go to sea baits. In contrast a sea bait is almost all silver, which probably accounts for its high success rate. I should perhaps point out that a suspender deadbait, allowed to rise up from the bottom a foot or two, does allow the darker natural baits like carp, perch and trout to be used. At present I am dealing with static deadbaits, fished hard on the bottom. The technique section will cover suspended baits.

Sea deadbaits are easy to buy from your local fishmonger. Mackerel, herring and sprat are the most popular, followed by smelt and sardines. Any of these baits can also be coloured by dye if you are fishing a hard water and need to offer the pike something different. You can also use pouting, whiting (I once had a 'double' on a really rank whiting), eel sections or any small silver fish. One of my friends, Jerry Airey from Essex likes fishing sandeels, so I took him to a local lake one winter morning where we took several jacks from the margins on this bait.

With large baits like herring and mackerel you have the option of either fishing them whole, or cutting them to fish with half baits. The fact that pike pick up half baits surely indicates they are scavengers, and spend a good deal of time moving around the bottom looking for dead fish. Sea baits in general will tend to be a lot softer for casting than naturals, so it is important to ensure they are frozen, and only thawed at the last moment. If they have been frozen hard in a deep freeze take them out the night before a trip and put them in the fridge. They should thaw out slowly. Better still

The author slides the net under a Savay lake pike. A long, carbon rod is essential for placing a bait on the gravel bars or drop-offs where many pike patrol. This fish fell to a deadbait.

take them to the bank in either a cool box, ASW Coolfish bag or one of those thermal silver sachets. You can then refreeze any baits you do not use, and be sure that those used for casting will still be frozen and allow a good hookhold.

Once sea baits go soft they are useless for any casting, and sprats particularly leave a decidedly anti-social smell on the fingers. Baits like smelt will tend to retain ice longer, and ice floats, so you may need to shot your baits down to make them sink. Far better to test them by lowering under your rod top, leaving the rod in the rest and the bait about a foot under. If it is too iced up it will float, but the moment it starts to sink you should cast out before the bait softens too much. Frozen baits cast like a bullet, and will certainly get you some extra distance in windy conditions. If you use half mackerel or herring you will find the tail section more successful than the head. I have had a few doubles on heads, but never a twenty pounder, yet I have no idea why this should be so. I have even fished two rods in the same swim with the baits a few yards apart. One with a tail half, the other a head — and still the tail gets more runs! The only theory I can come up with is that it possibly resembles a baitfish that has swum into a weedbed or bottom debris to hide: the head-in-the-sand syndrome.

Having mentioned baits going soft I should point out that these need not be wasted, and can be used to groundbait an area. Pike anglers have used sprats for groundbaiting for as long as I can remember. Certainly twenty years ago I used to bait Dogmersfield Lake heavily with sprats, by the deeper water of an old oak tree, and the corrugated tin swim. Even when I packed up from a morning session before work I would catapult out all the left over and discarded hookbaits. It worked to such an extent that if conditions were good I could expect a take anything from ten seconds to three minutes after casting in. After a hammering I was forced to change baits, but it indicates groundbaiting is a worthwhile technique, particularly on little or unfished waters.

Sprats can be fired out whole, but herrings and mackerel can be cubed up into three sections and thrown out. While primarily sight feeders, the pike can also locate baits by smell. For that reason I use pilchard oil concentrate as a bait additive, either smearing it on

Go Fishing for Pike

An Irish "double" explodes on the surface as the author fights it on a light bonefish spinning rod. The fish grabbed the bait just as it was about to be lifted from the water.

externally, or injecting it with a syringe. You can also make up a fine groundbait from mackerel meal and chopped sprats. This mixes into a very sticky, gunky mess, and is best employed as a means of groundbaiting an area out of catapult range. One mistake I have seen pike anglers make is to make the balls too large—they either burst open in mid air, scattering close in, or just cannot be fired out far enough. Mix the balls small, the size of a peach, and wet the pouch of the catapult before firing them out. This prevents sticking. You should also scatter them over a wide area. Remember they are concentrated smells and can dissipate in the water.

A tip to remember when distance baiting is not to fire out the balls first, then find you cannot reach them with a rod. You would be surprised how often this happens. Cast out with the size bait you intend using first, mentally mark where it goes, then catapult the balls out to the same distance. Alternatively if you have access to a boat, it is a simple matter to row out and drop the mixture in the predetermined area. Such prebaiting can be done after fishing sessions as you can then judge whether the area needs extra bait or not. If you are catching a lot of pike there is no need to bait. If you have dropped runs, or see pike moving but can get no takes, try prebaiting . . . it can soon spice up your pike fishing.

Moving on from regular deadbait colours you can now dye them bright colours: red, yellow, orange, green etc. This may be enough of a change to bring you that long-awaited run from a hard-fished water, but quite honestly if you cannot get a run on any of the aforementioned baits, I see little point in colouring them. Fish presumably see colours to a different degree or tone than the human eye, so there is no telling if a yellow sprat actually appears as yellow to a fish. I would suggest dying baits purely as something to do to entertain yourself, or to use if you have nothing else to lose. Quite honestly if you cannot get a run from any of the live or deadbaits mentioned, sell the tackle and take up golf!

Floatfishing

This section deals with floatfishing from the bank, which can of course apply to static fishing from an anchored boat. There are two reasons for bank fishing: you are either searching for pike that you *think* are present, or you are staying put in a hotspot where you know the pike are. Floatfishing fundamentally entails suspending a bait at a predetermined depth. My own views on this are basically that you need to keep the bait about one third of the depth up from the bottom. I have no scientific proof why this should be an optimum taking area, but my own catches show this to be the best depth. The only times I alter this are in early autumn when the fish are chasing fry on the surface when I floatfish about a foot or so beneath the surface, or in the depths of winter when the lake is about to freeze, and then I set the bait as near the bottom as possible.

You will also have to take into account what bait species you are going to use: perch, gudgeon, carp and crucians will all pull downwards for most of the time. Therefore in deeper water of five feet and more you can bulk the shot beneath the float and let the baits travel naturally through the lower surface layers. Bleak and rudd however may need a couple of swan shot pinched on the trace to keep them down, and prevent them from tangling the trace around the mainline. Avoid the old-fashioned toilet cistern style of float. The idea of supporting the bait is initially to do just that. When a pike pulls a float under, you want it to feel minimum resistance so it doesn't drop the bait. The pike bung offers the opposite to this and also requires a huge weight to cock it so I don't recommend it. Instead, buy yourself half a dozen long, slim pike floats. They will take plenty of weight whilst still offering minimum resistance. Today the modern pike float has a centre hole to allow you to fix a bead and stop knot for a sliding float rig. This is used in very deep water, where your rod is less than the water depth, and you cannot cast properly.

If you have no previous knowledge of a hotspot you would do well to cast as far as you can, and every five minutes, move the bait towards you. The bait itself will dictate its own direction, but once it has searched the extreme limit of your cast, bring it in closer. Should you wish to hold a small livebait in one area on a windy day, try degreasing your line with some diluted washing up liquid. Before you cast, squirt some on the reel spool and allow to soak

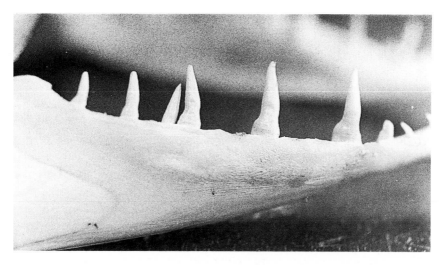

Close up of the main gripping teeth in a pike's jaw. Teeth like this are designed for holding, rather than cutting fish.

between the coils. Once the bait hits the water take a few fast turns holding the tip beneath the surface, and the sunk line will create a drag factor preventing the bait pulling away too much.

Should conditions be flat calm and you want the bait to cover as large an area as possible, treat the line with mucilin to make it float. Then when the bait has settled, throw a few loops of loose line on the surface so there is no drag factor, and to allow the baits to travel freely in any direction.

Very windy conditions mean you will need to change tactics slightly. If you want to anchor the bait in one area, sunk line alone will not be enough to prevent the bait dragging. You then need a paternoster rig, which basically entails a lead anchoring the bait and float in one position. You can still degrease the line because in a strong wind there will always be some sort of sub-surface drift.

Moving on a stage further. If you still want to floatfish, but you simply cannot cast to the area you want, then you must not only grease the line to make it float, but you need a special drifting float that sports a bright orange vane for visibility, and that will catch any wind. Years ago we used to stick a swan feather in the top of the float, which did pretty much the same thing. Using one of these fixed or trip-free vaned floats you can work a bait out as far as you want. That may mean 150 to 200 yards. Of course any spirited struggle on the pike's behalf is deadened by playing it on such a long line, but at least you get to slide the net under an extra fish.

I note that with a drifter style of float the vane might be in high-visibility hot orange. Why not paint the tops of your standard pike floats the same colour? Not only does a float serve as a bait suspender, but as a bite indicator as well. The faster you can see the bite, the quicker you can strike and the better the pike's chance of survival on unhooking. For pinching on swan shot to the line I have now seen an angler using a length of silicone tubing, with a small diameter enough for 12-lb monofilament to pass through it. This tube is about two inches long. He then pinches the swan shot onto the silicone tube, which reduces the chance of pinched shot fracturing the line. The alternative is to pinch the shot directly onto the wire trace, just below the swivel. On heavier floats a small drilled bullet might be better suited, sliding it down the line to rest against the swivel.

Any sliding float rig needs to have a bead and stop knot. The beads can either be the plastic variety obtainable from most tackle shops, or you can purchase your own on a cheap necklace which is cheaper. Simply cut the beads off the necklace, keep a few in your tackle box, and the rest in store. If your rod is fitted with large rings and the depth you wish to fish is about ten or twelve feet you can get away with the tiniest of the plastic ledger stops. They clatter through the rings a bit, but they can work. A better way is to buy some elasticated thread as used by peeler crab anglers for binding a crab to the hook. This can be overwound on itself and finished by several half hitches. It should make a moveable stop knot without fracturing the line. The third way is to use a proper stop knot using 5-lb line. Although not difficult to tie, it can weaken the line, and puts curls in it if slid to different depths using your thumbnail.

There are going to be occasions when you want to fish a paternoster bait over a weedbed, but keep the line clear from the bait. For this you rig up a sunken float paternoster using either a small polyball or a pilot float which is fixed up the mainline using a stop knot and bead. I dislike the white polyball and prefer a dull painted pilot float—if the white polyballs are used extensively on a hard fished water, the sight of them will eventually spook a pike. Whatever length you fish the wire trace, the distance from the swivel to that stop knot should be longer. Problems occur when the bait swims towards the surface where it can tangle the hook on the stop knot or bead. You may otherwise be unaware of this and only discover it when you strike and break off, the line having run through the pike's teeth. You will also get this problem occurring if you let too much slack line out. Then it can sink and the fish will drag the trace through. Also as the float is sub-surface you have lost visual indication of a strike. Therefore keep fairly tight contact with the pilot float, maybe even clipping the line to the rod butt. The weight of the pilot float can vary from a few swan shots up to two ounces or more. You need as much or as little as conditions dictate; the lighter the better, and I never worry too much if the tugging of the bait moves the weight very slowly. Stop knots are easily slid by wetting the line first, so depths can always be adjusted. Remember too that a deadbait can be effective when fished under a float, but that they work best in windy conditions, when the waves give the bait a bit of movement. Under these conditions I find the bait is best secured in the horizontal position with the holding or retaining hook set somewhere in the back to ensure the bait hangs evenly. I also find that natural deadbaits are better than sea baits.

Another tip when fishing floatfished 'deddies' is to try a single hook through both lips. This means the bait hangs tail down in the water, a most unnatural sight to a pike, but you can then twitch the bait via the float, and cause it to dart upwards. This added movement should be quite sharp, and repeated after the bait has settled for a minute or two. Keep all the shot away from the bait, as this would cause it to sink too fast after you have tweaked it to the surface. Bulk the shot under the float. The beauty of this method is that you can give some good movement to a deadbait, making it rise to the surface even at long range, something that couldn't be done without the aid of the float. If freelining, the bait would come towards you on a more horizontal plane. I also believe the action of the float disturbing the surface might attract a pike to the bait, and

I know a few specialists of this method who have actually hollowed out the nose of their floats like a sort of popping plug, to create more disturbance when they jerk the float. The same can actually be done with a liphooked livebait, especially when the fish are getting tired, or have gone to sleep. A short jerk will often start them chugging around again.

Freelining

This is a method that precludes the use of anything except the bait. I use it when waters have been really thrashed, and the pike are getting wary of anything with drag attached to it. The float goes under, the pike moves off a few feet, you get ready to strike. . . and the damn float pops up! Try casting out the livebait with no other weight on it. You will have to hold the rod all the time, and either retrieve loose line if the fish swims towards you, or feed it out if he wants to swim away. This can be a very exciting method of fishing,

A natural bait, rigged with a metal spinning vane, and pair of trebles for instant striking.

especially if you start to get used to one rod and reel. If you keep constant contact with the bait, without pulling it off course, you will actually feel it start to get agitated as a pike nears it. Livebait may refuse to swim in an area where there is a pike, so wind in and cast him out there. A take often comes immediately. It is similar to livebaiting a tuna for marlin. Then I can hold the line in my fingers and feel the tuna go crazy as one of the big billfish homes in on it. When live-lining for the mighty tarpon in Florida I hold the mainline in my fingers, linking me directly to the live mullet. You wouldn't believe how hard that mullet pulls just as it senses a tarpon is nearby. Often the mullet alone will jerk the line from my fingers. When they get twitchy like this we call them 'nervous baits'.

If you want to keep some retention on the area the freelined bait follows, you could slide a link ledger up the mainline, and stop it about ten feet from the bait with a stop knot. A livebait can still pull the shot along the bottom, but at least it slows it up a bit, and is far enough away from the bait to give it freedom of movement.

For deadbaits I call the method *twitching*. Years ago it was called sink-and-draw, but that was a fairly uniform raising of the rod top, fairly mechanical in movement. My way imparts a hell of a twitch to a bait, and it doesn't always get the chance to sink down again as I give it half a dozen twitches to jerk it about. The best bait of all for this is the dace, followed by roach or rudd. I have tried all sorts of multi-hook rigs, snap tackles and such, but now opt for my own invention called the "Lip-Clip". I also use this rig when deadbait trolling from a bait, described later.

To give the bait the best action, the point of pull must come directly from the mouth. If the bait is hooked anywhere else it will spin or create too much drag for a sharp tug. It also looks un-natural to a pike. If you have ever taken the trouble to watch a fish in distress, it goes into a sort of fit and flits about near the surface, and this is what you should try to imitate. A fish in its death throes, is one a pike knows he simply must have.

I always used to put two trebles in one flank and pass the end of the trace through the eye sockets, or out through the membrane of the lower jaw. To stop the bait folding up on the cast I pinched on a swan shot behind the jaw to take the impact of the cast. With a

The most recent fish landed by the author on his lip-clip rig was this superb 19lb 2oz pike taken on a bonefish rod, Shimano 4500 reel and rudd deadbait. Twitching deadbaits will be the mobile method of the future, and this specimen is the largest the author has taken using this technique.

laterally compressed bait like small bream or sprats I put the hooks in the same but passed the trace through both eye sockets, stopping it with a swan shot. The shot actually fitted very nicely into the eye socket. This was fine for big pike that engulfed the bait in one swoop. I could strike immediately and be fairly sure of a good hookhold. But on small to medium pike if I waited for the pike to turn the bait, which it swallowed head first, the hooks would be facing the wrong way, and have to be torn through the bait on the strike before they penetrated. The fault was noticed after I'd fought a pike for a few seconds, then watched as it opened its jaws and coughed out my hooks! You would be surprised how hard a pike can bite down on a bait, preventing movement of hooks on the strike.

I looked to my big game experience in marlin fishing to alleviate and improve the situation. With livebaiting for marlin, the bait was also turned and swallowed head first, but we use something called a bridle rig, which is a loop of 80-lb dacron about four inches long, attached to the bend of a large single hook, 14/0 in size. A crochet needle was used to pass the loop of dacron through the front of the eye sockets where it was half hitched to the bend of the hook again. This left the bait's mouth free to move properly, thus ensuring free flow of oxygen over the gills and a lively bait. When the tuna got eaten the hook folded round on the loop of dacron, and was then facing the correct way for striking.

My first attempt at adapting this rig for piking was in conjunction with trolling. I used a V.B Partridge single for hooking through the lips, but found it was too tight to the bait to fold round properly. Sometimes it even buried itself in the bait, a problem occasionally encountered when fishing for marlin. There was no way I could bridle-rig via a crochet needle, the smaller baits, yet I needed to have some space between the hook and bait, to allow free swimming movement for the bait, and clear hook penetration when the pike turned the bait. I tried two V.B. singles in tandem. One hooking the bait through the lip, the other farther back, so when the bait was turned I would at least have one clear for setting in the jaw. I caught a lot of pike like this, but the VB hooks have another small retaining hook on the shank. This is set at 180 degrees so

The author's own theory on 'eyed' baits came from his experiences when marlin fishing. Hawaiian boat captains say there MUST be an eye on their Konahead lures to act as a striking point for the marlin. Here the author has adapted his own "eye" to this sprat deadbait by using two contrasting colours of card, held in place by paperclip wire. (Please note the previous comment with the "Professor" lure having a bead that might possibly resemble an 'eye'.)

represents a flat hookholding chance.

The only hook that gave me an exposed point was the treble, which when laid against a bait would always have at least one point exposed—so I started using the V.B. single as the bait holder and a size 6 treble as the 'hooking' hook! It worked even better. Then I began to think about that bridle rig again, and how it really did give freedom of movement to the bait. I was also looking for a solution to bait flying off (I like to crush any barbs as much as possible). A bridle rig offered freedom of movement, but there was absolutely no way the tuna could shake it off. The answer came in the Graeme Pullen "Lip-Clip" (soon to be patented). The idea for this came when I simply filed a point on the wire end of an American snap swivel, and wired the eyelet straight on to the base of a size 6 treble

Two methods the author devised for rigging sprats for deadbait twitching. They can easily be used with other deadbaits.

hook, carrying the trace up through the treble eye for two feet to the barrel swivel. Either livebait or deadbait can be hooked through the top lip (you may need to bend the swivel wire into a more rounded shape), snapped shut and cast out. The swivel means the bait can move freely; it is impossible to cast off, short of tearing through the skin, and my treble is further back, so when a pike turns the bait to swallow it, the other points of the hook rest around about the bait's hard gill cover, thus making at least one point stand up proud. Do I give you exclusive tips or what? The "Lip-Clip" at present seems the answer to several problems, and I dare say somebody will improve upon it, or even bring out a treble hook with an extension clip to the base of it. I use this rig when twitching deadbaits and float trolling from a boat (of which more later).

Twitching

For twitched deadbaits you have to cast out, let the bait sink down, and watch the line where the bow enters the surface film. You can see when the bait hits bottom, and as soon as this happens give the rod top two or three sharp skyward jerks to pull the bait off the bottom, and make it jerk and twitch higher in the water. It is essential to keep the rod high, so you can give a drop-back to any fish. This buys you a couple of seconds to open the reel's bale arm to a taking fish, and prevent any pressure. When the rod reaches just before the vertical drop it, let the bait sink and repeat the procedure. What happens underwater is that the first pull makes the bait rise off the bottom, but not in a direct line to the rod top because it's likely to veer off to one side or the other. Your second tweak will snatch it back from that direction, and the third tweak, snatch it the other way again. This accelerated movement makes the bait flash and kick considerably, hopefully attracting the pike.

When you get the bait close to the bank, or if you are casting alongside deep margins you can actually tweak the rod with your wrist so fast the action on the bait will make it shimmy and quiver. You need to keep in contact with it to work properly, so try experimenting with these two methods in clear water. I learned many of my retrieves for predators from American bass fishermen, who are experts in the art of transmitting impulses down a fishing rod into a lure. They make us look prehistoric with our big baits, pike bungs and rod rests!

The most important point I can make about tweaked deadbaits is to suggest that through your skills you make the bait appear to live. You must be the bait. Let your 'mind's fingers' run down the line into the bait and use the rod just as an extension of your arm. If you tune in sufficiently, when a pike hits you'll get blown out of your socks with fright, especially if the take comes just as you have seen the bait hove into view, and you are about to lift it from the water. The same can be applied to lure fishing, but twitched dead-baiting is so close to being an art, the two don't bear comparison. As I said before, it may look in diagram form like sink and draw, but it is leagues ahead of that, and with livebaiting getting more restricted, the angler who learns this art well, will find little reduction in his catch rate. It may be difficult at first however, as you can only use one rod at a time.

Static Deadbaiting

Having dealt with freelining and tweaked deadbaits, we must now look at statics. Possibly the most mind-blowingly boring pike method of all time, it is also one of the most successful, especially for big fish. You can freeline a large deadbait at some distance, and let it rest on the bottom. That would be basic static deadbaiting. However this method allows a degree of slack line indication, and you could end up with a deep-hooked fish. Now you must use a ledger rig, not so much for added casting weight, but to make a point in the terminal rig that means line must be pulled near the rod to indicate a bite. A simple running ledger rig as shown is good, and means the pike only has to move a few feet before registering a pull on the indicators. If the weight of the bait is similar to the ledger weight, will 'helicopter' on the cast, and sometimes tangle. To alleviate this you should use a stiff wire boom as used by carp anglers, or make up your own with thin wire and silicone tube.

If you really feel happier with a freelined bait, at least attach a sliding float to give you some idea when a pike is moving off with the bait. If you are fishing over soft weedbeds the last thing you want is the bait to sink down and be masked. You have to suspend the bait in that weed in order to put it within the pike's vision.

My own catches show an increased number of runs when I use a buoyant bait over clean ground as well. There are two ways to make the baits buoyant. You can either cram the mouth and gullet with polystyrene, which is OK, but fiddly and not ecologically friendly, or better by far, you can pump them up with air using a hypodermic syringe. You may have trouble acquiring a syringe, as your local pharmacist is hardly likely to believe you are using it for fishing, but enquire when you next see your G.P. as he knows if you have a record of drug addiction or fishing addiction and can probably suggest an outlet. If you need some serious air in an oversized bait, try poking a long balloon down the throat of the bait, then partially inflating it. It looks like you are giving a 2-lb mackerel the kiss of life, but who cares if you put a 20-lb pike on the bank. Alternatively use a bladder syringe which is enormous, and puts the fear of God in most people. You could blow up a football with one of those.

Go Fishing for Pike

Having sown the seed of suspension in your mind, there is another way to view things, especially from the pike's point of view. You may think that a dead fish is just a dead fish. Not so. When something dies, becomes an ex-species, has expired, it gases up with decomposition. Not the most tasteful things to talk about, but I like to put fish on the bank, and that means learning all the small tips. Initially, when a fish is in its death throes it is twittering and skittering near the surface on its side. I mentioned this in livebaiting and deadbait twitching. When it dies it usually sinks to the bottom. It is then that the static deadbait looks the same as a naturally dead fish. Yet when that dead fish gases up with decomposition it will invariably have some sort of curve in the body through rigor mortis, and also start to float to the surface. From here it will drift into the windward bank, and rot away quietly on the surface—unless a pike gets him before that stage is reached.

There are three points you can learn from this and you can either combine all three, or use just one of them to adjust your approach. First, how about rigging a suspended deadbait with a pair of hooks, but placing the second set of hooks so that the body is curved? It will not be possible to cast excessively long distances, but the presentation will at least look like a 'natural' deadbait. Secondly, the gases in a dead fish mean the belly distends, which creates an imbalance in flotation and hence many dead fish are belly up. A live or dying fish is right side up, so surely a more 'natural' deadbait would be suspended off the bottom, in the upside-down position? I have been doing this for years, and again this is a tip I have not seen or read of elsewhere.

You need only suspend a deadbait from six inches to a foot off the bottom, but you can see my point of view that a living fish is unlikely to be hanging right side up about a foot off the bottom and completely static even when a pike nears it! Only if you have excessive bottom weed that might obscure a bait would I lengthen my trace rig to suspend a bait three feet or so up in the water.

My third tip is to take note of what I said about prevailing winds. If the wind has been blowing for more than three days in one direction, any dead fish that are inflated with the gases of decomposition will drift towards the rushes or bank into which the wind has

94

been blowing. Place your bait about three feet from the edge of that bank and you stand a good chance of connecting with a scavenging pike that will patrol that edge looking for dead fish. These then are three tips that might just start you thinking a bit, rather than merely throwing any dead fish with a hook in it, in the general direction of the water.

Another method I have used with deadbait is called the splash-attractor. I once saw an angler using it at Frensham Great Pond, when the pike were coming off fry-bashing, and would only pick up freelined deadbaits. You tie some one inch square pieces of wood onto the end of your line. No hooks, rigs or leads. About six little blocks are drilled through the middle, and a spacer bead put between each. The whole lot is cast as far as possible, then cranked and splashed over the surface to kick up a commotion. You start by fan-casting from the outside of your swim or area, gradually work-ing towards the spot where you want to present your bait. This is supposed to attract any slumbering pike into that area, and you follow up by casting in your bait. It sounds a bit crazy, but the angler in question had watched a TV programme about Polynesian fishermen who connected a string of sea shells together on a hoop, and thrashed them around on the surface to simulate a shoal of baitfish; they took enough fish over 20lb to avoid ridicule.

I use a similar technique myself on occasion, mostly in shallow water estate lakes and in colder weather when the pike might be a bit lethargic. If I have a hard frozen bait I cast out and retrieve from the same spot half a dozen times. Very occasionally I get a take on the way in, and several times I will get a run within minutes of casting the bait out. Certainly it doesn't hurt to cast baits out repeatedly in an effort to wake up any pike. I remember in Ireland they used to row the boat right through the edge of the rushes to push out any pike. That seemed crazy to me too—until I caught a few jacks doing it. Never discount anything until you have tried it.

On clean-bottomed lakes you can induce takes by moving the bait towards you. In autumn this can be a problem as the hooks will drag into any leaf and twig debris on the bottom. In winter, when the bottom should be cleaner, you can bump the bait towards you, but do it violently with a good hard tug to move the bait about

The author with a big double-figure Irish pike taken from a boat on Loch Muckno. This water is ideal for trolling techniques.

three feet at a time. I mentioned before how I had sat up trees at Dogmersfield Lake observing pike staring at static deadbaits for hours on end. Twitch them and they will often grab it. This method can be even more successful if you twitch a suspended deadbait. This way you avoid any bottom debris being picked up on the hooks, and if you use a heavy lead like a 2-oz bomb, the bait should dart downwards and then rise up.

Trolling

Of all the different methods I use for pike, twitching deadbaits is one of my favourites, but for sheer bliss give me a day trolling. Maybe it's being out in a boat that makes it so exciting, as you can poke about in inaccessible corners of lakes that you might not be able to reach from the bank.

There are two types of trolling: that done with deep-running lures and a downrigger, or that done with baits. You could argue that

This Japanese trolling board works on a similar principle to the planer, and can be fitted with these Aftco line release clips.

lures and baits should be put into two different categories, but this is how I personally divide them. Dealing with downriggers first, when running a boat and streaming lures out behind you, you are dependent on the action of that lure to determine what depth you are going to cover. In large waters the baitfish and pike may be in a restricted or stratified temperature layer, and only a lure pulled through that depth will catch. Many lures imported from America sport a long vane on the chin which makes them run deep. The problem here is that you need to run a boat with outboard power in order to pull the plugs fast enough to make them dive. There is no way you can pull the same plug slowly and get it down far enough.

A downrigger system consists of a lead ball, either circular or bomb shaped, attached to a wire line. Near the lead ball there is a release clip into which you clip your reel line, having measured off a predetermined length to the lure. The lead ball is lowered to the depth you think the fish are. When a pike takes, it pulls the line from the release clip and you can play it from the rod as usual. This allows you to pull a lure slowly and still maintain the correct level.

However, a point many anglers forget is that the plug itself, if a diving variety, will run below the stratified temperature level you have selected. If for instance you set the downrigger ball at forty feet, and put out a deep diving plug, it may well be that the finished depth is over fifty feet.

Also from my experience of downrigger fishing at sea, I find the fish, especially predators, strike *above* their field of vision i.e. a predator likes to rise in the water to take its prey rather than dive down towards it. Therefore if the bait strata is at forty feet, you would be more accurate in running the downrigger at thirty feet, and allowing your lure to pull the extra ten feet down to run slightly above, or in that bait area. The alternative is to set the ball at the bait depth and fish with a big flashing spoon that is likely to fish more on a horizontal plane. You can also use a rigged bait in place of the lure, but I feel you need to run more slowly with baits, and a

Boat fishing for pike is certainly entertaining. It enables you to reach spots you might not get to otherwise. Here the author eases in a nice pike for the camera.

faster running boat with a lure enables greater ground to be co-vered. On a large water that you may have no experience of, you would probably do better to cover as much ground as possible with lures, and then fish baits when you have established a productive area.

The alternative to downrigging is the use of wired or lead-cored lines which help to push a deep-diving plug down further. These can be quite effective to get to the slightly deeper levels, but for forty feet or over, I prefer the downrigger system. The pros and cons of cored lines will always be argued, but there are two points worth noting. The cored line will be non-stretch so your chances of dragging the hooks of a big lure in past the barb are increased. However that same non-stretch quality will work against you when the fish gets near the boat. Monofilament nylon however stretches around 10% and this can be a safety margin when a big fish surges near the boat. With a non-stretch line the safety margin is reduced, and unless you adjust your drag to suit, there is every likelihood that you will tear the hooks out on cored line. It is all very well saying you will remember to adjust the drag, but with a big double or twenty pounder starting to surge away from the net, many can forget, including me!

Float-Trolling

While I like any sort of trolling because you are always covering potentially exciting new areas, the slower method of what I call float-trolling seems a peaceful exercise. This can be done from a powered boat, but unless the prop blades are small and engine revs reduced to a low tickover, you will probably pull the baits too fast. The heaviest bag of pike I have taken recently was in Ireland. I managed 100lb of pike with five doubles, all taken by this method. Using a bit of muscle power with the oars you can also pull baits through very shallow water, something you cannot do by outboard. Pulling a deadbait behind a moving boat is nothing new. "Trailed Herring" was a standard technique, but I like to think I have refined a technique that was previously fairly basic. Float trolling is for use in waters up to fifteen feet deep. Anything deeper requires a downrigger/cored line approach. From working on waters of about forty acres or more I found a hooking rig on both livebait and deadbait increased my takes considerably. Gone are the days when I used the odd bit of deadbait trolling to kill a couple of hours. Now I go out with this one technique and find it is my basic method of catching pike on the larger waters.

The deadbait is mounted with the "Lip-Clip" described in the twitching deadbaits section. Instead of clipping the deadbait through the top lip, it is best to seal up both lips; the action of pulling it through the water will close the lips anyway. Having done that, the main problem I came up against was finding a way to add some movement to my deadbait. When deadbait twitching from the bank, you can simply jerk the bait to move about. Fishing from a boat on your own however, means the oar work keeps your hands occupied, so you are basically dragging a dead fish through the water. So I turned to my saltwater trolling experience and decided to de-bone and split-tail the deadbaits. To the uninitiated, and that will probably be most pike anglers, the removal of the backbone means loss of rigidity in a bait, and in this instance, good movement when pulled through the water. With saltwater trolling you are pulling baits at anything up to 7 knots, but I could still see how this technique could be applied to my piking. My American de-boning tool was too big for freshwater fish, so I opted to fillet out the backbone. This allowed some movement, and I found the pike took the softer bait much better. I could also set the hooks quicker.

The split-tail technique involves filleting out the backbone, but slicing an *exact* split down the centre of the bait, ensuring the split carries on between the rays of the tail fin. Only if it was done like this would the bait run straight, and it is quite a tricky operation if you haven't done it before. Use only the sharpest Normark filleting knife to split that tail fin. I use the "Lip-Clip" in conjunction with a size 6 treble hook. No need for multi treble rigs.

The alternative is even better. You tow a livebait through the water on the "Lip-Clip", but clip them only through the top lip to ensure constant freedom of movement and flow of oxygen over the gills. The same size 6 treble is used. I use the float to control the depth of the bait, and to prevent it swimming too deeply. Most of the time I want it in the top three or four feet of water. A rough guide would be to set the float with a sliding stop knot above *and below* the float to hold it in position. That way if you are fishing more than the length of the rod you can wind the float over the lower stop knot so it slides down onto the trace swivel. If the depth of the water is four feet, set the float at six feet. Remember that as soon as you move the boat along, the bait will rise up and be pulled higher in the water. To compensate for this, bulk your shot either above the swivel or on the wire trace itself in front of the hook.

I like a nice steady rowing speed, just enough to keep the baits pulling in a straight line behind me. If the water drops off deeper and you can isolate this area with an echo sounder you can actually slow the boat and allow the baits to work deeper, right down to the six feet if you have set the float at that. Hold them there for a while, then row away hard for a few oar pulls, dragging the baits upwards hard, which usually makes them thrash about. More than once has this created or induced a take.

Two people can fish three rods. I start by running out the distant line first, then set one a bit closer in, and maybe I put a third straight off the stern, running a few feet back. I also use a weight or anchor, as on a windy day you can soon drift into rushes, tangling your other lines when you hook a fish. I lay a rod out at each side of the boat, either in those gunnel rod clamps (secure a lanyard!) or leaning them against the seats. You must remember that even though the baits on either side will be spaced apart say, twenty feet, when you put them in the water, they will get closer to each other the farther you run them back. Therefore as I run my distant bait at least fifty yards back and the second at about thirty, they will often be in a straight line. On a large open water the third rod can be slotted about ten yards back.

I also believe the action of the float creating a vee-shape as it cuts through the water might arouse the interest of a pike, especially when followed shortly after by a sparkling, wriggling livebait. The takes when float trolling can be savage! I now use a sailfish release clip. This again is from my saltwater experiences where you need an immediate drop-back to a sailfish that takes a bait while trolling. They have an adjustable screw and a tension release that can be altered to suit the individual. I can then fish with the bail open. Trolling a live fish tensions up a rod quite substantially, and it will pull round to a set curve. You will learn to distinguish snags and weed if you try to watch the rod tops as much as possible. A snag means the rod drags round slowly and steadily. On a windy day it will soon pop the release clip, but a taking pike will have more of a kick to it. Only experience will tell you the difference. If you have any doubts about whether a bait is weeded or not, wind in, clean and run out again.

It is important to remember to run the baits out while the boat is moving. Start rowing, drop a bait over, leaving the reel bale arm open. Let it run back forty or fifty yards, drop it in the release clip. Run out the second bait to the required distance, inside the first of course, and put the line in the clip. With two of you aboard, one can row while the other tends to the rods. Run a third short, straight off the stern. Once set, a fourth rod could be implemented for lure fishing, but quite honestly float trolling is so good I doubt you will need it.

Other than the vee-shape the float makes on a flat calm day, you are otherwise unlikely to see it. You must remember you are not using the float for signs of a take, but to prevent the bait swimming too deep. I have been experimenting with a variety of vanes, and I hope I have come up with a hinged float that can fold over to a taking fish. It's not important to the technique, just a minor refinement. I am sure somebody else can come up with a better idea.

When rowing along remember that the floats may not necessarily follow the same curve you do. If you have a snaggy bay and you need to drag the baits as far in as possible, maybe running them near to overhanging tree snags, you can grease the line which then makes them skate over the top of the surface and "cut the corner" of the boat's wake, thereby avoiding the snags.

On the other hand you might want to really 'put them in it' and need to drag baits round on a wider curve. Degrease the line with washing up liquid and the line then has friction with a bigger area of water and tends to follow the track of the boat better. I should perhaps point out that on a water of less than fifty acres with fairly intricate snags, bays and headlands, you can get into an awful mess

Techniques

if you are a poor oarsman. If doing float trolling for the first time take a partner. You can take it in turns on the oars and rigging the rods is easier. Remember too that pulling out of a curve will make the outside bait swim a lot faster and therefore ride higher in the water. You may need to slow up when coming out of a curve to keep the speed of the bait constant.

Float trolling can almost become obsessional, and I hope some of the big pike specialists may try this technique. It is a lot more interesting than sleeping in a bivvy all day at some desolate pit waiting for your deadbait to be picked up!

Striking

Striking is another topical subject. Decades ago pike were allowed to run for minutes until they were gut hooked. Gorge-baiting it was called. Thankfully that is now a thing of the past. I can still remember the old "smoke a cigarette first" technique of striking. Certainly you wouldn't do that today, not if you want to put the fish back alive. Much depends on the size of the bait: A small jack with a half pound bait might run yards with it held crosswise in its mouth. You strike, and get a lacerated bait back. Next run you leave it a bit longer, only this time the fish is a double and on banking it you find the hooks have gone down its stomach. Small wonder hooking pike was deemed a problem.

I now look at it this way. I already have stated I refuse to use big baits. Therefore anything that I strike at and miss, probably isn't worth striking at all. If the fish is over 6-lb I consider it a worthwhile catch and it should have the hooks somewhere in its mouth. If you tighten down to a pike, while holding the rod high and watching the tip (keep the bale arm open!), you should see the heavy taps on the rod tip as the pike turns the bait. If the taps are small and slow with just the occasional heavy bump I find it is a good fish, and then I thump the hooks home hard, and quickly. If the tip taps and tweaks about quickly I find it is a jack pike having trouble turning the bait. A big pike only needs a few fast jaw movements to throw even a moderate bait down its mouth. If you are fishing minnows and bleak for fry-feeding pike, you can hit them almost immediately; no more than ten seconds. If there was an optimum time I would say maybe 30 seconds is enough, although I admit that when pike are finicky they can hold a bait crosswise in their jaws for over a minute and then you can still miss them on the strike.

It is rather like shark fishing. If a fish is screaming off line and doesn't look like it's going to stop I hit it. Those ones are usually small fish, spooked by drag, and they will drop the bait anyway. The ones to be wary of are those that either move very little or move off slowly and steadily. They are the bigger fish, and should be hit sooner. Much depends on your experience and trial and error; everyone will get a deep-hooked pike sooner or later through no fault of their own.

Night Piking

I feel a mention should be made of the opportunities that exist for the angler wishing to stay out all night. For my own part I can honestly say I have only done a few all-nighters, and you need to be a fairly hardy individual to spend all night on the bank in December and January! While I dislike the go-to-sleep-in-the-bivvy style of fishing, I think this really is a situation where you need to get in the sleeping bag, zip it up and get some sleep. The pike are unlikely to go wild and hit the baits in droves. More likely you can consider it a result if you get one fish. This is primarily dead bait fishing, and you need to use the back biter alarm indicators if you do intend sleeping. That way you are immediately aware of any slack-line bite occurring, and can minimise the chances of a deep-hooked pike.

Pike in the dark must surely locate food by smell, which again indicates they are scavengers. I cannot see them hitting a live fish in the pitch dark, so they skulk along the bottom in search of dead fish. For this reason I avoid using suspended deadbaits, and prefer to fish them hard on the bottom. Use plenty of concentrated fish oil either injected into the bait, or smeared onto it. I use Brent's concentrated pilchard oil. You might also wish to put some sort of visual attractor on the bait. Try those small chemical lightsticks called Cyalumes manufactured by the Cyanamid Company in America. They are a small plastic phial that carries two separate chemicals. You bend it to crack the internal phial thereby allowing the two chemicals to mix, thus creating a very bright light. The two best colours are red or green, and in cold weather they will last all

Night piking is mainly for the dedicated, but it does occasionally produce good results. Large, single fish are normally the order of the session, rather than lots of smaller fish. The author with a Dogmersfield "double".

night. If you only intend fishing a few hours into darkness, you'll be pleased to know you can preserve the light by freezing the cyalume phial in the fridge. That way you can use it again another night.

There is quite a bit of scope for night piking in summer, which nobody seems to do. Presumably this is because there are so many more species to catch at night in the summer. I feel it would be more productive than winter night piking though. The largest pike I personally know to have been caught on a summer's night was a 24 pounder, and certainly it seems to be the larger pike (from double figures upwards) that make a showing then.

You should consider the use of cyalume lights in front of lures in failing light. I have used them myself with limited success. I believe there is now a plug on the UK market that carries a slot for putting in either lightsticks or scent attractors.

Tackle

You could almost write a book on everybody's idea of the perfect tackle for piking. It really is largely dependent on the individual, and exactly what style of pike fishing he is likely to pursue. For deadbait fishing where you want either a heavy bait casting, or to set the hooks at long range, you will need something a bit beefy. Try the Sportex 12-foot carbon-Kevlar with a 3-lb test curve. There aren't many baits you can't throw with that model. Ryobi have a Super Specialist 12-foot rod with a 2-lb test curve. That slots into the average bait range and would suit most anglers. Tri Cast have a 3-lb test curve carbon rod, 12 feet long, and that is a good heavy caster. Keep a look out for the new Shimano range of pike rods which are due in 1990 sometime, they should be a high-standard casting tool as well.

For me the only reel of top quality is the Baitrunner Aero range. Their new range will be set to take the long distance casters by storm. With a long spool, and immaculate line lay, they will definitely push baits out farther. They are great for casting lip-hooked livebaits into the wind. Using a finer diameter carbon rod like the Ryobi Master Pike, with through action, and coupled to one of the new Aero reels you will cast further, with less effort.

For deadbait twitching I like the Biomaster range by Shimano, and the drag is ultra smooth for playing fish. I also use a very old Cardinal 54 by ABU for my light tackle deadbait spinning. It sports a good stern drag, and is light and easy to hold all day. On the boating scene you can look to the standard stern drag range marketed by Ryobi. They are competitively priced, and stand quite a bit of punishment when trolling or plug fishing. If I had a perfect outfit for most livebaiting and lure fishing opportunities it would be the Ryobi Master Pike—a superb action rod for a very competitive price. The largest fish I have so far landed on it was a 50-lb plus Nile perch! Coupled with a Shimano Biomaster it makes a balanced outfit that is hard to beat.

Lines are simple. I use Ande Tournament in the green 12-lb breaking strain for everything. It is soft and supple and seems to have a good spool life. For hard wearing durability it seems the brown Sylcast takes some beating. I find it stiff compared to my Ande, but I still use it when distance fishing for bigger pike in gravel pits where the bars and drop-offs might chafe an inferior line.

Weighing the fish is done in one of the shop-bought weigh bags used by carp anglers. Weigh the pike in as near a horizontal position as possible. I cannot see bending a double-figure fish does its internal organs any good. Make your weigh point around the middle, rather than either the head or tail. For scales there are only two types, both dials, the Avon or the Kevin Nash are the best, with an easy-to-read face.

For me, Partridge hooks are the best, both with their range of trebles and the V.B. singles. Between them they will suit most anglers. I use them in conjunction with Marlinsteel stranded wire, but there are other ranges of wire available. For indication you can use any of the modern Optonic or Viper sounder alarms, in conjunction with any of the various indicators available. You are unlikely to be hitting a six-inch twitch bite, so I therefore advise the use of the two alarms that register drop-back bites. You can buy the ET Back Biter alarm indicator or the Gardner Drop-off indicator. They are both good and solve problems of slack line indication. They are especially good if deadbaiting when you are likely to doze off in the periods of inactivity.

The days of floats like huge ballcocks bobbling around are surely numbered. I use them mainly as swim markers. Now you can buy streamlined customised pike floats to suit a wide variety of techniques and conditions. The Kevin Nash vaned drifter, or the ET drifter float are both good for drifting live or deadbaits out. Kevin

Tackle

Testing out a new Ryobi Specialist carp rod is Adrian Hutchins. Although designed for carp, they make great rods for double-figure pike, as the bend will indicate!

Go Fishing for Pike

Nash also markets a loaded weedbeater for float fishing, which is ideal for holding station in choppy conditions. Pike Tech market a streamlined sunken slider float for paternoster rigs, and moving water, while the clear streamlined Drennan range of floats, is great for small livebaits.

Forceps, wire cutters, scissors, gloves, and degreasers that slot in the butt ring can also be bought over the counter. If you buy a landing net get a big one, some have a large mesh at the top to be able to sweep through the water quickly, and a close, fine mesh at the base for cushioning the fish. Pike are best returned as soon after capture as possible. You can try the carp sacks, or if you want a catch or large-pike picture, use a very, VERY big keepnet. I have four between twelve and fifteen feet long, and on the rare occasions I do put pike in them for a photograph, it is for only a short period. They are perfectly OK if left in the water, but it is the constant dragging out and throwing back that damages them. Leave them alone and quiet, although I appreciate that can be difficult on a heavily fished water, or one the public has access to.

Remember the pike is our biggest freshwater predator. It receives more angling attention today than ever before, despite the fact that years ago many were instantly killed. There were less anglers fishing for them then, and they certainly didn't have the technology the modern pike angler now has at his disposal. More than ever, the future of maintaining a good head of pike for sportfishing lies with the beginner or young angler.

Pike fishing can be great fun, so enjoy it, but help preserve it for the next generation . . .

GO FISHING FOR

GO FISHING FOR
TROUT
GRAEME PULLEN

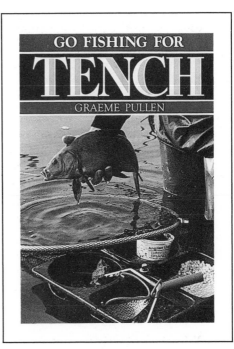

GO FISHING FOR
TENCH
GRAEME PULLEN

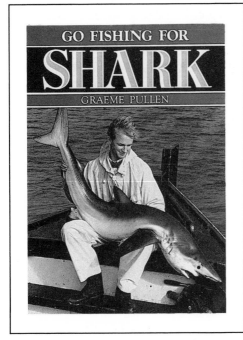

GO FISHING FOR
SHARK
GRAEME PULLEN

GO FISHING FOR
COD
GRAEME PULLEN